SAMUEL

Samuel Baldwin

ISBN 978-1-63844-268-4 (paperback)
ISBN 978-1-63844-269-1 (digital)

Christian Faith Publishing, Inc.
832 Park Avenue
Meadville, PA 16335
www.christianfaithpublishing.com

Printed in the United States of America

Inspired by God!
May all the glory go to God in the Most High.

ACKNOWLEDGMENTS

W ITH GRATITUDE TO MY *loving family—my wife, Lisa; daughter, Colette; sons Sam and Michael; and my sister Sunny, for meeting me in the living room that night in 2016 and sharing their hearts.*

Special thanks to my sister, Sunny, and brother-in-law, Tom, for always being there for me through steadfast prayers and support.

To our very good friends Sue and Jim M., for their encouragement and enthusiasm for this book from start to finish.

To my mentor Jim B. and friend Grant G., along with many other friends and family for their prayers and support along the way.

To my family for all the editorial help, especially from my grandson Logan for teaching me some of his creative writing skills.

CONTENTS

INTRODUCTION

WHY READ THIS BOOK? It is a true story about a boy called Sam later to become a man called Samuel. It is loaded with pitfalls—bad decisions due to erratic behavior and irrationality due to the mental effects of drugs and alcohol. This story can be interesting, intriguing, insightful, encouraging, and full of hope.

Many people can relate to many aspects of this story. It is also packed with spirituality and the work of God in his life for a period of over fifty years. It's a message of God's grace despite his rejection of him and the many years of destruction he left behind. He also points out the power, progression of drugs and alcohol, and the lack of ability to recognize the reasons for failure and destruction.

The rise and fall of his financial house was cyclical and sure to happen again. For him, it seemed, about every ten years, there would be a major failure, then smaller cycles every two to three years; but it always ended in a financial collapse. Some of this is due to an untreated mental condition exaggerated by drugs and alcohol. This book also tells about the saving grace and forgiveness of Jesus Christ. It also tells what great lengths God will go through to bring him back on track and shape him for his work and his glory. The end of this book is only the beginning. There will be more in the next book. Sam's life was exciting and very eventful, but when the dust settled, life had very little meaning. And the reasons were greed, selfishness, love of money and material things, and avoidance of God's will with rejection. Money and material things have always been a wedge between God and man. Also in Sam's story, he spent months wandering in the wilderness with very little direction, hopeless, and with no clear path for any kind of a future. During this time of wandering, all of Sam's needs were met daily. All the years of drugs and alcohol were being sweat out. During this time, God was remolding Sam and preparing him for a new purpose.

CHAPTER 1

Influential Events

A WHITE CAR CROSSING THE centerline headed straight at me. I was just twelve years of age, pedaling west on a secluded country road and hugging the right side of my lane. Even though I took a near ninety-degree right turn into the ditch, the white car could not be avoided. So as we collided, the bike went under the car while I flew over, landing headfirst on a small tree, penetrating my forehead.

While all of this was happening, I was asking myself, *Why was this white Ford Falcon station wagon after me*? I had never seen this car before. What did this person have against me? Fearing for my life, I attempted to jump up and run, not knowing about my badly broken leg and ankle. Instantly, I passed out and became temporarily unconscious.

When I came to, a big teenager was walking toward me. I was scared, face and body covered in blood, and leg and ankle twisted behind my back. Being helpless, I could barely move.

The young man looked at me, stunned, and said, "What happened to you?"

I looked right into his eyes and said, "What the hell do you think happened? You just ran me down."

Now he had driven 220 feet after running me down and hit a telephone pole, and he then awoke. He had been up all night drinking. Heading home, he had fallen asleep at the wheel. His car was full of beer cans, I was told later. He didn't even know what he had just done, so he really wasn't chasing me after all.

By this time, other cars were stopping at the scene. A very nice lady, an off-duty nurse, came over to comfort me and helped the best she could until an ambulance arrived. Pain was taking over; I was yelling and crying, "I'm deformed. I'm deformed." My face was a mess. Under my nose, it looked like there were two golf balls between my upper teeth and upper lip. My upper lip was ripped halfway up under my nose. I must've looked hideous. My face, forehead, and ankle were gushing blood; and my leg twisted like a pretzel. Even in the present condition, I was conscious enough to be very upset about the damage done to my new yellow Schwinn Varsity ten-speed bicycle.

My name is William Samuel Baldwin. Born in 1960. This is just one of the numerous events throughout my life in which God spared my life for a greater purpose later in time. These events helped shape my character, some good and some not. I was raised with five brothers and two sisters. During this time, Dad was a high school teacher; Mom was a stay-at-home wife. And they were also foster parents. Mom and Dad were devoted Christians. Our lives revolved around the church—Sunday morning, Sunday night, and Wednesday nights. Even while on vacation, Dad would find a church for Sunday morning. Not all bad, the church was filled with wonderful people that cared about all people and did their best to mentor us in God's ways. But sometimes, I still got tired of going so often; sermons were long and strong at a young age.

Our family was somewhat dysfunctional. The house had revolving doors and alternating shifts for meals. The house was maxed out when fully occupied, so everyone was coming and going. Dad was gone a lot—church functions, teaching, or schooling—so Mom was very busy just trying to keep up with her workload. There was quite an age gap between the younger and the older, so our schedules were all very different. We also had a family paper route for *The Blade*, which most of us worked on, including Mom and Dad. So things were hectic, and nothing was consistent except school and church.

Now I was a high-energy kid, a bit mischievous, and always looking for the next best thing to do or accomplish. I probably had ADHD, but they didn't know what that was back then. I wasn't stupid; but I didn't do well in school—couldn't slow down, pay attention, and be interested. I was good-natured, got along with others pretty good, loved to play, and was willing to do just about anything that sounded fun or adventurous. But at school and church, I felt like an outsider, with the way we dressed and the cars we drove. I wore hand-me-down clothes. The only time we got new clothes was birthdays and Christmas, and they weren't up to current styles. Most of the time, I didn't care, but I hung around kids that grew up similar to me.

Now the only one younger than I was my sister Jane, just a couple of years younger than I. Jane was a good sister and daughter. Jane always wanted to please her parents. She did well in school. She followed the rules, and she was a hard, diligent worker. Jane was generous and helpful anytime she was needed. She was also athletic; she ran track. She was strong and tough. She had to be in a house full of boys. I wasn't always nice to Jane. I think I envied her relationship with Mom and Dad. To Dad, she could never do wrong, so I usually got the blame deservedly. Ben was my brother, just a couple of years older than I. Ben and I got along great most of the time. But I knew exactly how to push his buttons to get him really mad. So I would do that to him just because I could. Then he would chase me down and pummel me. But all in all, I learned a lot from Ben, good and bad. Ben was bigger, tougher, and more skilled than I at everything; but he always looked out for me and defended me. I was always his little brother; he was always there for me when I needed him. Ben and Jane were the ones I grew up with because of our closeness in age. But going up in age, there were Pete, Dick, Sunny, John, and Bob. I was proud of all my brothers and sisters even if I didn't always show it in my words and actions. Most of them were moving out or moved out as I was growing up.

Now we also had up to seven foster kids living in the house with us. Mom and Dad were compassionate and really wanted to help these unfortunate kids. They had come from all kinds of backgrounds with all kinds of problems. Some didn't stay long, but some stayed for years. We would all get attached and would have a hard time when they were gone. Some I played well with and hated to see them go. All my brothers and sisters were intelligent, independent, and hardworking. That was how we were raised. Most of them went to college or a trade school and did well. I was also very independent and stubborn. I was going to do things differently than all of them and do it my way.

Mom and Dad had huge hearts. They were good, caring people. I think they wanted to do more than they really could. They did the best they could raising us—teaching us good morals, not to be afraid of hard work, and to persevere. We didn't have a lot growing up unless we earned it, and we did. We all worked hard, and we accomplished much. Mom and Dad always went all out at Christmas. They did their best to supply our personal needs and fun stuff too. The foster children were part of the family and were treated generously. None of us were properly equipped for some of these children, but we all did the best we could. All in all, our holidays were always good and warm.

These years raising foster children were especially hard on Mom. It really pulled on her heartstrings, what some of these children had gone through, and she kept most of it between her and Dad. Some had parents incarcerated; some were starved, malnourished, abused, locked in closets, and retarded—all kinds of mental and physical issues. It was a lot on Mom's and Dad's emotions. But we loved them; they were family. We got attached, and it was hard when they had to go back. These were tough times for Mom. She had times of depression, and when foster care ended, she was happier. When that was over, she went to nurse's training and became a nurse at fifty years of age. She worked with premature infants until she was seventy. I think those were the happiest years of her life as far as I knew.

Now I had a passion for fishing, and so did my friend Ed. Ed and I would fish every chance we could from early spring until late fall. Neither one of us had much money for tackle, so we would walk along the riverbanks and bridges looking for tackle other fishermen would leave behind. We would make poles from sticks and wrap the string around the ends. We'd use nuts, bolts, and even rocks for sinkers and, many times, rusty hooks. We actually caught lots of fish on those stick poles, and it was fun and challenging doing it that way. But of course, we desired to have modern, efficient, and newer equipment.

Sometimes we would travel miles on bicycles or on foot to fish new spots. We both had a lot of freedom as kids. Our parents were glad we made good use of our time. We weren't really very skilled because nobody really taught us. We would ask other fishermen questions to get whatever tips we could. Sometimes they acted annoyed at our questions, so we would move on. So we mainly used worms and crawdads when we could afford them. We would use home-built rafts with poles, maneuvering up the creek and fishing from the banks.

When I was eleven years old, I pedaled my bicycle about three miles to the local hardware to look at their fishing equipment. I was only planning to look so I could get some ideas. I really liked the golden Eagle Claw hooks, so I suddenly got the idea I could take them. So while looking around, not seeing anyone, I stuck them in my pants and headed for the door.

Now I didn't know I was being watched through a one-way glass up high. Before I was able to exit, the store manager stopped me. He told me he had been watching from his office and saw me put the fishhooks in my pants.

So I fessed up, gave him the hooks, and said, "You can have them back. I'm sorry."

He said, "That's not good enough," and sternly invited me into his office.

Wow, I could see the whole store from up there; but by then, I was crying, afraid of the consequences, whatever they would be. Then he called the owner of the store, and we waited for him to show up. When the owner showed up, he said he would call my parents. I cried harder and pleaded I would be in big trouble. So he said, otherwise, he would call the police, and I'd be prosecuted. Now I didn't know what that meant, but it didn't sound good. So I gave in and gave him my phone number. So he called home and talked to Dad, and he would be on his way. Boy, I was scared. I knew Dad wouldn't be happy about this. Dad showed. He was calm, and he apologized for me and assured the owner that I would be properly punished and it would never happen again.

So I was released to pedal back home. I didn't hurry too much because I knew I was gonna get it; plus my bike only had one pedal. The other had broken off, making it difficult to go too fast.

When I arrived, he was waiting for me at the front door and signaled for me to enter. After I entered, he led me down into the basement with his big paddle in his hand. The paddle was hard dark walnut, about three and a half inches wide and three-fourths of an inch thick, made by his high school students in shop class. Dad was a teacher at Waite High School and was familiar with unruly teenagers. Once in the basement, he had me lie on the concrete face-first. He then proceeded to beat me with that big paddle. I didn't understand the furiosity of his anger, but I didn't think he would stop. I know I was screaming and moving around, attempting to avoid the next hit.

But he said, "If you don't stop moving, I'll hit you harder."

So I just screamed, yelled, and cried as loud as I could. When he was done with my backside, he flipped me over on my back. Then he proceeded to hit me on my face, not with his fist, but with his palm and back hand. Dad was a big man with big, hard hands, and it hurt bad. When it was finally over, the only thing he said was, "No son of mine will be a thief." After saying that, he got up and headed upstairs, leaving me to lie there. I lay there weeping and crying for a while, then went into the den which was in the basement to lie down.

During this time, Mom had been upstairs hearing the whole thing. She never said a word and never came to rescue me or console me. Mom never would say anything against my dad's actions or decisions. Now I believed I deserved the punishment, but I also knew it was extreme. It was difficult to even sit down for a week. I was bruised from the middle of my back down to my calves. My face was red as a beet for quite a while and bruised bad enough I didn't want to see anyone, but I was also grounded. Neither Dad nor Mom said a word about the punishment until after my accident a year later.

Something happened to my spirit and my trust after that day. I don't believe I held a grudge toward my parents, but it changed me. It broke my happy-go-lucky spirit and hardened my emotions. The things that were very important to Mom and Dad were not important to me anymore. At church, a couple of years earlier, I was taken into a classroom during service and whipped with a belt for squirming in church pews. So now I started to hate church and everything it stood for. Internally, I changed. I felt alone emotionally and wanted to grow up different than my parents. I decided I didn't need school, and I didn't need church. I was independent, and I would determine my own destiny. I loved Mom and Dad, but I was reserved and guarded. I did deserve to be punished, but it did change me and not all for the better.

After that, Dad never did hit me again, and we didn't talk about it. I never understood what led to his extreme anger that day. Now I know Dad had a tough childhood and upbringing, but I didn't understand the impact of it until I was much older. When Dad was about nine years old, his brother, about fifteen, died. His brother's name was Walter, and he had been sick his whole life. Walter's father was a doctor. He did everything in his power to save his son's life. After Walter's death, my grandfather was so distraught that he took his own life. The same day, my dad's grandfather had a heart attack and died.

So in a very short amount of time, Dad lost three of the most important people in his life. I can only imagine how his own mother must've taken the loss. But one thing's for sure—my dad went through an awful lot of heartache and pain at a very young age. As a kid, I had very little knowledge of my father's childhood and no understanding of what he went through. After that, he went to live with an aunt that didn't really like kids. Later on, he needed to take care of his mother. While my father grew up, he spent a lot of time alone, so he did a lot of reading. He was very good in school, a highly intelligent young man.

So after high school, my father joined the air force and became an officer. This was just in time for World War II. In the war, he was a navigator and bomb raider. Now he was scheduled for a mission across the ocean with his unit. Just before he was set to go, they pulled him from that flight and ordered him to teach navigation school. If he had been on that plane, I wouldn't have existed because their plane was shot down, and all dad's comrades perished. My father had been through another really difficult and trying time.

When my father and mother met, they wanted a large family, and that they did accomplish. But neither one had experienced raising a large family. Now I've raised my own family, and I realize that, after the circumstances of both parents, they did a great job.

My mother was a country girl growing up, happy in an average upbringing. She just had one brother. But Grandma came from a very large family, and Mom had lots of cousins. Mom was very devoted to her husband; she followed him with a trailer from base to base while he was in the air force. My brothers Bob and John were born during this time and traveled with Mom. My parents were true patriots. They loved America and sacrificed much so I could be free and grow up in peacetime. No matter what differences I had with my father, I deeply admire him for his patriotism and the sacrifices he made in his lifetime. But he still overcame much adversity and exceeded all expectations with honor and greatness.

On August 6, 1973, about 11:00 a.m., I planned to pedal my bicycle to my brother Bob's to mow his lawn. I had bought a brand-new Schwinn ten-speed varsity sport, and I welcomed the opportunity to use it. I had saved up most of the money to buy it. Dad loaned me the rest. Bob had a riding lawn mower with a big yard, and he would pay me to do the job. So off I went, taking a country road with low traffic. I believed it to be the safest and fastest route, and my parents agreed. It would be about a six-mile ride, but that was no big deal to me. I rode all the time. Now I had gone almost one halfway, on my right-side lane, when I noticed a white Ford Falcon drifting my way. He was moving pretty fast and heading straight toward me. As I pedaled onto the shoulder, it seemed he was intentionally coming right at me. With a big open road ahead of him, why was he coming at me? But why had I never seen this car before? And I was just a kid with no enemies. So I headed into the ditch, but the collision was unavoidable for me. He then struck me head-on. I cartwheeled over the driver's side fender, landing headfirst into the ditch, while my new bicycle was crushed underneath the car. After I was struck, I thought he was after me, and I attempted to get up and run. But because of the shock and pain, I had gone temporarily unconscious. I was unaware of a crushed ankle and a badly broken leg. When I came to, my face was covered with blood. I could barely move but saw a man walking straight toward me. Shaking uncontrollably and scared, I looked at him, awaiting for what would happen next and still thinking he was after me for some reason.

After the awkward confrontation with the hungover driver, I was angry but too worried about my own predicament and soon forgotten he even existed. Cars were pulling over and plenty of help was being offered. The off-duty nurse stayed with me until paramedics showed up; she was a sweetheart. Later we found out she had gone through nurses training with my mom. God was shining his grace upon me. She was calm and professional, and the fear of being chased had evaporated.

After about twenty to thirty minutes, an ambulance and paramedics showed up. By this time, the real pain was setting in. You know, at first, I didn't really feel a lot of pain; but the blood and damage to my face and body just scared me real bad. When the paramedic put an air splint on my leg, that hurt really bad. I had never experienced anything in my life so far that came even close to comparison. I was an active, accident-prone kid since a toddler. None of that was anything compared to this. The ride to the hospital was very uncomfortable. I moaned and cried all the way there. But I still asked, "What about my bike? Is someone going to get it?" I worked hard for that bike, and now it looked like a pretzel. But I wasn't ready to give up yet. The man in the ambulance reassured me someone would take care of it for me but said it doesn't look too good, and that really upset me even more.

Shortly after I arrived at the hospital, much of my family was also getting there. I'm sure they were all very worried. Mom, Dad, and my brother Bob were with me in the examination room. The doctor was a very kind, patient man who was making several attempts to set my leg bones to no avail. This was more than I could handle as I cried and writhed in extreme pain. During this, I was very worried about my face. My upper lip looked like it had two golf balls in it.

I could see my lips. I didn't need a mirror. It was ripped halfway up under my nose. My forehead had a deep gash, and also my left ankle, gashed. My entire body was splattered in blood. All this was very scary to me. Finally the doctor said I would need surgery to set my leg, so he put a temporary cast on it unset. This was a little relief, but I was a mess and just wanted the pain to stop. After that, they gave me a shot, and I don't remember much for three or four days after that. What I do remember is waking up in pain until another shot and going right back to sleep.

For this part, I was hospitalized for better than two weeks. They were able to set bones, but it was a very jagged break for both bones. By the time I was lucid again, my face was looking better, and swelling had gone down. I don't know how I ever could've handled the pain without the shots, but they had to wean me off. I never realized how painful a broken leg could be, but it was a time in my life that never left my memory. And it was something that I didn't cause to myself. Yet this experience, unchosen, would change the course of my life. Of course, at this age, I didn't know or understand this. Only now as an aged adult looking back on this experience could I see how one course of events change the next course of events. Life seems so simple, yet it can become so complicated.

In the second week of being hospitalized, I was awake more. Pain was subsiding, and I had a roommate also with a broken leg and also hit by a car. The kid was coming back. We shot spitballs. We were allowed to use wheelchairs, get snacks from the small kitchen, and move around a little. Mom and Dad were there every chance they could; and I was flooded with cards, flowers, and balloons. My parents and family were wonderful during this time. Mom and Dad both felt terrible about what had happened to me. Dad told me I had enough pain for a lifetime and promised to never hit me again. Dad kept his promise. He never did ever hit me again, but Dad always kept his promises. I'd bet later that he should've never made that promise. My family was a big part of my making it through this nightmare.

When I was finally released from the hospital, there was a party waiting for me at home. It was difficult for me to be the life of the party. I was very uncomfortable and still needed pain pills. The man who hit me also showed up with a card and candy. I wasn't very glad to see him, but he didn't stay long. Never saw or heard from him again.

I spent a month in a wheelchair. Not to take any chances, they wanted me still. This was also very hard for a twelve-year-old. All I was able to do was lie around and be waited on. Mom was wonderful. She took great care of me and would get anything I asked for.

This wasn't the end of it. The doctor said three to six months for the cast; that seemed forever to me. But after six months, the doctor said it wasn't healing, maybe another three months. So I started eighth grade, then my thirteenth birthday, and still a cast. This was depressing. No sports. I did a lot I shouldn't have done with a cast and had some falls on my leg that probably didn't help. I also got really fast on crutches, but this wasn't the life I planned on.

Then the bad news. After nearly a year, my doctor said I would need surgery. This was devastating news, but what other choice did I have? So I was back in the hospital, this time for a bone graft. This operation recovery was just as painful or more painful than the original break. I couldn't believe I was going through this again. They cut the top of my tibia off and installed five stainless steel screws attaching to the good bone over the gap. Back to shots and pills again and two more weeks in the hospital.

Again, this was not the kind of pain easily forgotten. Three months later, I was hospitalized again for a week due to complications caused by screws in the bone. So the screws were removed. The pain wasn't as bad this time; recovery was quicker.

Three months later, my cast finally came off. I was so excited. I thought finally I would be able to walk again. I was shocked when I saw my leg, skinny as a toothpick with hair one and one half inches long. I was afraid to even set it down on its own weight. Recovery was gonna take a long time, this I could see. My left leg was more than one-and-a-half inches shorter than the right. I would have to wear special shoes and would still be on crutches for a while. I hated the shoes. They were terrible, with no style whatsoever. One heel was extra thick with special arches.

I was on crutches into my sophomore year in high school. When I was able to walk again, it was with a bad limp. They called me clubfoot. During these years, I learned to self-medicate. I didn't take gym until senior year, and I still couldn't play any sports. But I learned to drink beer, and I loved it every chance I got. I had a full-time pass to the corrective gym, but I used it as a way to skip school. I skipped school a lot in my junior and senior years.

Mom and Dad didn't do much when I would get in trouble. I was suspended for ten days for getting caught with beer at a football game. I thought I would be in big trouble, but they didn't say much. I think, after all I had been through, they kinda gave me a pass. These were very discouraging years I went through. When I was better, I wanted to make up for all I had lost. I was gonna have fun. The young man that hit me didn't have good insurance because he was high risk, but they gave me all he was covered for. Now I couldn't touch the money until I turned eighteen, but knowing it was there and growing with interest was a good feeling. When I turned sixteen, I started jobs to have spending money during high school; but I knew, when I turned eighteen, life would get better. So I worked, and I partied. Life now was about having fun, and I was living life to the fullest.

My first job was bagging groceries at the local grocery establishment. A lot of my friends worked there also, and we got free beer. If a case of beer was broken, it was discarded. So after work, we would conveniently retrieve it from the dumpster. Now I justified it as not stealing because it was thrown out anyway.

Now I had several different jobs in high school, but I always worked somewhere. My senior year was a fun year. I skipped a lot but still managed to graduate. We went to lots of rock concerts. My parent never knew. I came and went as I pleased at home. Dad would argue and disagree with my lifestyle, but I would walk out the door and not come home sometimes more than a week. So there wasn't much my parents could do anymore. I refused to go to church very often. I only cared about myself and my friends. Also, my brother Ben and I were very close because he lived the same lifestyle. When my license was suspended, he would give me his.

Now, to back up just a little, by the time I was fourteen years old, my dad was very successful in his accomplishments. He was an English professor at the University of Toledo, and he retired a lieutenant colonel in the air force. He had accomplished much in his life. He was very knowledgeable in many subjects, such as history. We would have conversations lasting for hours about anything I could think of. He was highly respected and a very fluent public speaker. He was also a pilot, owned his own planes, and loved to fly every chance he had. Dad worked hard his whole life. He was a good father, husband, and friend. He wasn't perfect; but he was humble and faithful to God and lived by principles established on honesty, truth, and morals given by God.

He'd experienced many misfortunes, heartaches, and pain in his life which also shaped his character. So I hold no grudges for anything that happened between us in the past, and I know he held no grudges toward me.

Now it was wintertime. I was fifteen; we lived on a frozen creek. Dad had decided to land his plane on the ice and come up to the house for a cup of coffee. So he told me to skate down the creek and alert kids a plane would be landing. So I did. He landed and stayed about one-half hour. I cleared again, and he took off with no incidents. When he returned from the airport, he told me he would let me drive his electric Volkswagen on the ice. Dad was ahead of his time. He converted a 1960 Volkswagen to electric. It would go about forty miles per hour but only about fifteen miles on a charge, but I was impressed with what he had accomplished that many years ago. He also believed in recycling. We recycled newspaper, cans, and garbage and made our own trips to the dump once a month. But anyway, he drove through the park to get to launch and onto the ice. Once on the ice, I took the wheel; he showed me how to drive it. I did good, so he said, "Just go ahead and drive it home." It was just around the corner from the park. When we arrived back home, the local police pulled in right behind us. He could see I probably wasn't old enough to drive but asked me for my license.

Now Dad was pretty smooth and not easily scared or intimidated, so he invited the officer into our home. Dad was calm, humble, and persuasive and convinced the policeman to let us slide and then thanked him. As the officer was leaving, he told us he was still tracking down the crazy nut that landed a plane on the ice earlier that day. Now we all had to work hard to keep a straight face while discussing this with the policeman. But he left, and we never heard about it again. We all had a good laugh when he was gone and thought it quite ironic. That incident came up often at family get-togethers. It was a good memory and time when we were proud of how Dad would handle himself in this kind of situation. And there were many through the years with eight kids, and we weren't the conventional kind of family.

By the time I was fifteen, the idea of driving fascinated me. My parents were done with foster parenting, and Mom, at fifty years of age, became a nurse. She worked the night shift with premature babies. She really loved her work. When it was cold, being a helpful fifteen-year-old son, I enjoyed warming her car up at night before she went to work for the 11:00 p.m. to 7:00 a.m. shift. She really appreciated leaving at night in a warm car. It was fun for me because I would go back and forth up and down the driveway. Now we lived on a dead-end street. As time went on, I got bolder and drove a couple of houses down and turned around in a neighbor's driveway. Then I would drive to the corner, turn around, and come back. Sixteen seemed like a long time to wait to be able to drive.

When school was out, Mom and Dad flew out to California for a month to spend with aging relatives. Mom and Dad were way too trusting and naive to an overly ambitious teenager. A month is a long time to leave a fifteen-year-old boy on his own. We lived in a safe neighborhood, so Mom always left the key to her car in the ignition. To me, this temptation was just overwhelming. This car was a 1965 Plymouth Barracuda with an automatic transmission. One day, my good buddy Mark was over, and we were talking about the situation—parents gone and key in the ignition. I told him I was thinking about taking it for a ride. Mark was an instigator and said, "Okay, let's go." So we agreed, early the next morning, we would do it. Mark, always true to his word, was knocking on my bedroom window at 6:00 a.m. We needed to go early so my sister Jane would be unaware. So we took it out. I drove, and we were gone about one-half hour. It was very exhilarating getting it up to seventy on the back roads of Michigan. Our adrenaline was flowing as we made it back with no incidents.

This was not a good thing because I was emboldened and so was my friend Joe. While they were gone, I took it out many more times. Also my friend Joe started sneaking his dad's car out late at night. We would push it out of the garage and down the block before starting the engine so they couldn't hear. We got away with this for a while. Then one day, I was driving the Barracuda fast around corners when it started making a loud noise under the hood. So I got it home right away and parked it. When I attempted to open the hood, it was rusted shut. I was unable to get it open, so I left it until my parents got home. Now I was worried. How would I explain this? When they had returned home, Mom tried to drive her car, but it wouldn't start. Dad came out, worked on it, and finally got the hood open. He couldn't understand how the battery ended up on the fan blade.

So being the thoughtful, helpful son I thought I was, I offered my scenario. "You know, Dad, Mom is a zippy driver. She takes corners fast, and maybe she didn't know it happened before you left for California."

Well, I was not sure Dad was convinced, but he went along with it and fixed her car. So I was off the hook for now. I sure had learned how to lie and deceive. I felt guilty about it but not guilty enough to fess up to the truth. So I learned to lie anytime it was convenient as to not get blamed for my actions. So I continued to sneak Mom's and Dad's cars out every time I had the chance, and I got bolder and would take them out even when they were home. So sooner or later, I was gonna get caught, and that's what happened.

So one night, I took my dad's Toyota pickup out for a joyride. My good friend Ed was in the back hootin' and hollering as we came flying up the street. There was Dad standing there, waiting at the end of the driveway.

The first thing he said was "How fast does it go? Did you have it over one hundred? I think it's time for you to go home, Ed."

Wow, I couldn't believe I was caught, or maybe I couldn't believe I didn't get caught sooner. I knew I was too old for a spanking, but there would be consequences for my actions. So I was grounded indefinitely, and he said that I wouldn't get my driver's license until I turned eighteen. Wow, what a blow. I didn't see that coming. That was the end of borrowing cars for me, and I was on my best behavior for a while. Not getting my license at sixteen was devastating to me, so I knew I needed to make drastic changes. And I did. Dad had given plenty of chores and projects while I was grounded. One of the chores was to clean the basement, and that was no small job. Years of a large family and the basement was a convenient place to throw things. I spent several weeks in the basement, cleaning and organizing everything. I painted all the walls and the floors which had never been painted before. The basement was better than it had ever been. Then I did the garage. Mom and Dad were very impressed and happy about what I was able to accomplish when I put my mind to it.

I completed the garage and did a lot of yard work with no complaining, and I had a good attitude. I was impressed myself. I think it had all been really good for me, and Dad never had to raise his hand toward me. They figured I learned my lesson. When I turned sixteen, I got my driver's license. Also Mom bought a different car, and the Barracuda was given to me as my first car. What did I learn from this? Did I learn to manipulate to get my way? I did learn I could accomplish a big project when I put my mind to it. This experience didn't change me. I did what I needed to do to accomplish my goals with my wants being a priority. I was determined to drive at sixteen no matter what I had to do. Mom and Dad were hoping this had straightened me out, but this was just the beginning for me. I just learned how to lie, manipulate, and convince Mom and Dad that these things weren't going to happen anymore. I just became more sneaky and worked harder to put on a good front, and I would do whatever I had to do to get what I wanted.

CHAPTER 2

Unrestrained Teenager

Well, turning sixteen and getting a license, at least now I was legal. All the driving I did illegally, there were no incidents other than being caught by Dad. If I had been caught or gotten into an accident, I wouldn't have driven for a long time. Within my first year, I had two accidents and two speeding tickets. I guess I wasn't a very good driver—too fast and not paying attention. So my license was suspended for a year because of too many points. One accident was a block from my home. I ran through the yield sign and broadsided an old man. The other accident, I rear-ended someone. Both were my fault. So for a year, I pedaled, walked, rode a bus, or bummed rides to school and work. I did have a moped which I used a lot, but I stayed legal this time as to not jeopardize my driving again. My luck driving legal was worse than when I was illegal. I was determined. I still made it to work while my license was suspended; I never missed and was on time. After getting my license back, insurance was an issue for my parents, but they took care of it and didn't say a lot about it. After the suspension, I was a careful driver, and no more tickets for a while. Not driving was embarrassing for me and difficult to date. When I was driving again, partying was first, work was second, and school was last. During the school year, we skipped school as much as we could get away with. During the summer, we used small boats and went to nearby islands for days at a time.

At the islands, it was a big party. Many would go. We had big fires. We would drink and smoke day and night. We would go regardless of weather—rain, snow, or freeze. We'd pull sleds and drive our cars and trucks on the ice. Nothing would stop us from our partying. One year, my friend Gary and I were determined to go in February, and the only thing we had to use was a canoe. The trip out wasn't too bad. It was cold and windy, but the wind was at our back. We had a great time that night. With a huge fire, there was no problem with the cold. But through the night, it got very cold, and the wind picked up. The wind was still going the same direction, which meant we'd be going against it returning home. When we looked across the bay, there were whitecaps, and the waves were over two feet. We had not planned on staying more than one night. We both had obligations, and we were out of food and beer. So we had to head back. So we headed across the bay. It took all of our concentration to keep heading straight. We both understood well that, if we capsized, we wouldn't survive; so we gave it all we had. We were both discouraged and worried. As we made it to the mouth of the river, it had frozen during the night. But there was no turning back now. So we decided it would be thinner in the middle, so we headed into the ice. At first, we were breaking through it; then when we got about a hundred yards in, it got thicker. It wouldn't break, and it nearly capsized us. Now we were stuck in the middle, ice all around us. If we backed out, that could be just as dangerous. We were stuck, and nobody was around to help us. Neither one of us were panicking, but we were concerned we might not make it through this. So we decided to just go slow and try to get closer to shore, even if we have to abandon the canoe. So that is what we did—slowly toward shore, breaking ice a little at a time. We eventually got the canoe ashore and walked back to get the truck to pick up the canoe. After the excursion, we were shaken for a while but also very excited. After these things happened and were over, I then wanted the next best adventure and excitement.

We were both very thrilled with what we had just accomplished, but we didn't do that again. We had defied death. We nearly capsized several times, knowing we would not survive trying to get to shore. Even though I didn't deserve it, God protected me again and brought me out of what seemed to be an impossible situation. But my party life was still first, and I was an adrenaline junkie. This was still just the beginning of many adventures. Every weekend was something, and I had plenty of friends that enjoyed the same things.

I was fourteen when I acquired my first boat. The boat had been sunk and frozen under the ice for the winter. Two guys dug it out of the river onto shore with plans to restore it. Once on shore and getting the water out, they decided it was more of a project than they were looking for. The boat was nothing special, with a large hole in the bottom and half-full of slimy black mud.

Well, I just happened to be there watching the excitement when one of the guys said, "You want it, kid?"

So I responded with "Sure, I'll take it," not knowing what I was getting into.

I was ambitious and unafraid of work. So I went home and had Dad come back with me. Dad wasn't afraid of work either. He helped me get it home and flipped over. After that, he used the numbers on the boat. After calling Columbus, we found the owner. We called the owner. He told us it was ours and gave us the title. So I was a proud owner of my first boat. It was a sixteen-foot wooden boat, very heavy but structurally sound. Dad and I had an agreement: as long as I was legal, with all safety equipment, I could use it. I cleaned the mud out, patched the hole, and sanded and painted the whole boat inside and out. I found a friend of my brother Ben who sold me a twenty-two-horsepower Scott-Atwater outboard engine for $28. It was a bargain. The engine ran great for many years. We lived on a creek with a dock, so I docked it in front of our house. I and my friends used it a lot. We would take it far out onto Lake Erie. We'd use it from spring to late fall—fishing, camping, and skiing. We had a lot of fun and became experienced and comfortable on Lake Erie. We would come back in storms many times with quite a bit of water in the boat.

These experiences only excited us, and we believed we were veterans of the lake. One time, we were coming back from the lake going full speed up the creek when the engine literally jumped off the back of the boat. It wasn't bolted on because there were times we needed to remove the engine and put it in the front of the boat so as to balance the weight so we could get under the bridge. Sometimes the water level was high, and the engine wouldn't clear the bridge. Anyway, when the motor jumped off and we stopped coasting, we paddled back to about where it jumped off. I could still see air bubbles coming up. So I jumped out, and believe it or not, I landed on the engine. There were three of us, so we managed to hoist the engine into the boat. We paddled about one-half mile back and took the engine up to our garage. I removed the spark plugs, turned the engine over to get water out, and put oil into the cylinders. The engine started right up. So we put the engine back on and were using the boat the same day. All in all, it was a great first boat. We used it a lot and had a lot of fun. But after two or three years, I had my eyes on another boat. A few blocks down on our street was a sleek smaller mahogany four-seat speedboat with no engine. This boat was just sitting there unused for a couple of years. It needed some work, but nothing compared to what I had done.

Finally, one day, I knocked on the front door; and the owner of the boat came to the door. So I asked him if he would be interested in selling.

He said, "Make me an offer."

I didn't have a lot of money. I worked but had car expenses.

So I said, "How about one hundred? That's all I can afford."

Well, he accepted the offer. I was very excited this would be a really sharp boat. I restored it. The top and inside were varnished natural mahogany. I painted the sides white and the bottom red. I installed my Scott-Atwater engine which would push this boat faster, and that I really liked. The boat was sweet. It even had a windshield with cushion seats that snapped off and on for maintenance. But this boat was a riverboat, not a good lake boat, but that did not deter me. It was much faster, maneuverable, and stylish.

So one of my best friends, Ed, who also enjoyed some adventure went along with me for a trip to West Sister Island. West Sister was about twenty-five miles from the boat launch into deeper, rougher water. West Sister is a wildlife refuge and not for public use. But we were only planning on being there for a couple of hours. We launched at daybreak. The water in the river was as smooth as glass, and the forecast looked good. But going into Lake Erie always has some risk. Storms and high winds come up fast. I had never even taken my bigger boat to West Sister, but I was confident with my boat-handling skills. We figured we'd clip quickly out there, and we started out good. The little boat was much faster than the other one. By the time we made it to the harbor light, the waves were two to four feet high and we were not quite halfway there yet. Two to four feet waves were doable, but we were getting wet. But the waves were getting bigger and bigger, and so was the wind. It was sunny, a little cloudy, but no rain or storms. Now we were more than halfway but couldn't go directly into the waves, or we would plow under because this was a speedboat, not a lake boat. Soon the waves became six to twelve feet; we were surfing the sides and the tops. When the waves would come together, I'd switch direction so we weren't heading straight toward the island. At this point, the island was visible but still miles off. We were moving along quite successfully using this strategy. I was standing up to get full control while Ed was sitting on the back of the front seat.

Just when all was well, Ed said, "Look at that big fish."

So I looked. Big mistake. It took my attention away for a couple of seconds as we plowed into a huge wave. The wave sent a wall of water over the deck and right at us. The water shattered the windshield, threw Ed into the back of the boat, killed the engine, and filled the boat half with water. We were both stunned at first, but we took action after I said Ed grab the frisbe and start bailing. As he started bailing, I went to the back to get the engine started. Now the old engine didn't have a cover over the carburetor and also no recoil. The water washed into the carburetor and drowned the engine. Waves were washing over the side while I looked for the rope under water somewhere on the floor, I found the rope, set the engine choke then pulled hard. It didn't start the first time, but this engine had never let me down. So I wrapped the rope and pulled again, and the old Scott fired up. I ran up front and started steering and gave it throttle. Meanwhile, Ed kept bailing. This time, I paid attention. It was still a long swim to the island. We were heavy and off-balance with all the water, but we both stayed on task—Ed bailing and me driving. At this point, I was feeling confident we'd get there if I continued working as before and paying attention.

Then we saw a much larger boat coming toward us. As he got closer, I could see he was having a hard time also, and the boat looked like a twenty-eight-footer.

Then we heard a megaphone, and a voice said, "Do you need help?"

Ed jumped up and said, "Yeah, we do."

But I said, "No, we're fine. Heading for the island."

So he said okay and waved.

Ed and I argued for a little bit, but I said, "Come on. We're almost there. We'll make it."

About an hour more and we hit the beach. We were relieved but also excited that we did actually make it. So we dragged the boat out onto the beach so it could dry out. We were safe, but our lunches were ruined. We didn't prepare for this, and we were hungry. So we figured we'd go fishing. So we took our lines, explored the island, and attempted fishing. We had no luck. We could see fish, but they wouldn't bite. After a few hours, we decided we would have to head back. We weren't prepared to stay. So we started to get ready to head back, checked everything out, and organized the boat. We had enough gas but no windshield, so we knew it would be a wet ride.

We waited until about 5:00 p.m., and the lake was calming some. The waves settled to two- to four-footer, so we left the island. Ed rode in the back and covered up with a tarp. I drove as fast as it would go. It was a choppy, windy, and wet ride; but I never slowed down a bit. And we made it home before dark. All in all, it was a fun adventure. We were glad to hit dry land and were cold, wet, tired, and hungry. But we were young, strong, and very excited that we accomplished another successful voyage. This was just another one of the death-defying adventures where God spared us and didn't get the glory he deserved. I stole the glory and called it skill, luck, and perseverance. That may be so, but it was by God's grace only.

Another adventure we enjoyed as teenagers was driving our cars on the frozen rivers and lake. Bunch of us would pile into our cars, head out into open area traveling at high rates of speed, crank the steering wheel, and set the car spinning around and around. Sometimes, when we were sliding sideways, hitting crushed ice, it felt like we'd roll; but we never did. We had a lot of fun, yet it was a little scary, never knowing for sure what would happen. Drugs and alcohol were usually involved. Yet we were fortunate nothing bad ever happened. While living these wild years, I was still very motivated by money, so work was part of most weekdays. Working probably helped to keep me from some of the trouble I may have gotten myself into. From my accident when I was twelve, a trust fund account was set up by the court which I was not able to use until turning eighteen. So it made it so I didn't need to save money for college because, when I became eighteen, I had over $10,000. This caused me to be reckless with money, so it really wasn't good for me. But I didn't care. It was nice to know going through high school and something to look forward to.

So in my senior year, my dad and my brother Bob knew I needed some plan for education after graduation. Also they were quite aware of my wild party life with local friends. They thought getting me out of Toledo would be a positive decision. They also took into consideration my natural abilities and the skills that I had acquired while repairing my own mechanical equipment through the years. I had rebuilt the engine in my car successfully when I was sixteen. I changed clutches and did my own brakes, bodywork, and anything that needed to be done. I wasn't much of a student in high school, but I got As in all shop classes and even in drafting. I was top in the class. When something interested me or it was fun to me, I did very well.

So Dad asked me if I'd be interested in pursuing aircraft mechanics. I thought it sounded really good especially when he told me where I would need to live. So Dad and I flew to Pittsburgh.

We both loved flying, and we had a great trip, landing at Allegheny Airport. He let me do most of the flying as he pretended taking a nap. It didn't matter; I was comfortable just knowing he was there. Dad was a good pilot and a great navigator, so I always trusted his abilities. Navigating a trip like this was elementary for Dad, being this was his expertise in World War II. Anyway, the school was at the airport walking distance. Arrangements had been made, and we toured through the school. It looked exciting to work on airplanes, smaller aircraft, but large engines and jet engines. It was all new to me, and I was impressed. Dad didn't waste time.

He said, "Are you interested going here?"

He told me he would pay my tuition but I would be responsible for apartment, books, lab materials, and tools. So I would need a job and to work through school. Back then, new encounters and travel sounded exciting to me, and I welcomed the change of scenery. So we filled out the application, made arrangements, and flew back home.

So the plan was in motion. I was scheduled for fall after high school. Dad had to sign because I would still be seventeen when starting school. Also, the first five weeks was probationary. If you didn't pass, you couldn't continue. Also, the entrance exam was three tests—mechanical ability, mechanical aptitude, and general ability. So I needed to pass those first five weeks. But the challenge sounded exciting to me, and moving out of state was also exciting. Dad and Mom were hoping I would straighten out some, and I did for a while. Somehow I did manage to graduate high school. I needed to for aircraft school. Minimum requirement was a diploma.

Well, knowing I'd be moving out and coming into money, I wanted freedom and adventure after school was done. What a great feeling when high school was finally over. Dad and I weren't getting along that good in my senior year. Minimal was all I did; I skipped a lot of days toward the end. We didn't see each other very much. Every night, I was at the bars, and sometimes I didn't even come home for a week at a time. I worked always no matter what my party life was. We traveled to the islands every chance we had. The party was always lined up for after work, and I didn't need much sleep. There were helpers for that too. Some parts of my teenage years was just a blur. I was always going somewhere. We also went to as many rock concerts as we could squeeze in. So really, it's difficult to keep all events in order because of my frame of mind during these times. Yet somehow, I always made it to work on time and did my job. So I think I was ready for a change. Moving to Pittsburgh might be just the right thing, so I thought. But I think I was in a rut and needed to get out. I was traveling down a dead-end road fast, and I had very little interest in listening to wise counsel.

So I made another plan for the meantime. The same day I finished school, I quit my job. The next thing after I cashed my check was to get packed up and leave Toledo just to get away for a small adventure. I really didn't like that job anyway, so I enjoyed quitting. I pulled my money together. I had $600, so I wouldn't be driving. I decided I would hitchhike down south. I didn't know where; I'd decide on the way. All loaded up with my backpack, I said goodbye to Mom and Dad. They didn't seem very surprised at what I was doing.

Dad said, "Make sure you take your Bible and read it when you can."

Mom said, "I love you. Be careful. We'll be praying."

They didn't have to let me go because I was seventeen and looked sixteen. But it wouldn't matter; I would go anyway. I didn't listen to Mom and Dad much anymore. Being I looked so young, being robbed did concern me, so I hid money in various different places. I kept some in my wallet to look like it was all I had, but I taped cash to the bottom of my feet inside my socks. I walked to the expressway nearest to my house and stood on the ramp. I was a free spirit. I felt free with no fear, but I was still careful about things that didn't look and smell right. My first ride was a truck to Dayton. I walked all the way through Dayton and picked up my next ride north of Cincinnati. My next ride was a traveling photographer. After we got to talking, he said he was going to Myrtle Beach and said I could ride the whole way. So I thought Myrtle Beach sounded like a good destination. Mike traveled a lot alone, so he enjoyed company. So in my first night, he let me stay in the motel room. So the next day, we made it to Myrtle Beach and parted ways as he went to work.

So I headed down to the beach, first time I had ever been there. Walking down the beach with my backpack and no particular destination was surreal. As evening settled in, I looked for a place to camp and hid out in a rest area. So I only stayed for a day and headed out. The trip home was not easy—lots of rainstorms, walking, hot sun, and sleeping along the side of the road wherever. It wasn't as fun as I thought it would be, but it was an experience. The boredom and sleepless nights I wasn't going to admit to anyone else. I walked many miles going home. Rides were difficult to get. I decided, next time, I would drive something. But God kept me safe. No mishaps. But I never read my Bible. Needless to say, I was glad to get back home, and I agreed with myself that I'd never do it again.

When I made it back home, I bragged what a great time I had. I spent the rest of the summer preparing for my next adventure. Dad bought a 1972 Subaru for $175. It didn't run, but it had low miles. So we figured it should be repairable. So I fixed the Subaru, fairly inexpensive problem, and put tires and brakes on it. The Subaru was very economical. It was so light I could lift the back end three inches off the ground. So in late August, I packed up the Subaru for the trip to Pittsburgh. So I only had clothes and tools, not much more a seventeen-year-old has. And of course, I left Toledo at night, having really no idea where I was going; but I had maps. This was kind of thing I really enjoyed, a lot of unknowns. I came into Pittsburgh from the south not knowing how bad the roads were in Pittsburgh. The roads were terrible—huge potholes, very hilly, and winding. It was late at night coming through, and when I hit these huge holes, it felt like the car would break in half. I found my way to the school by early morning before they opened. So I rested until they opened, then went in to get information. When they opened, I went in and introduced myself. They were very helpful, gave me a list of apartments and job prospects. So I left after calling and setting up appointments with apartment owners. Back in those days, there were no cellular phones, so it's either using available phones or pay phones. So after looking at a few, I didn't care about fancy or perfect location. I wanted cheap. I was very pleased with my selection—a twenty-five-minute drive from school, third-floor efficiency, and fully furnished. It even had dishes, pots, and pans; and the rent was $100 a month including heat. Not bad. Water pressure was not very good, hot in summer, and no air. Previously it was a funeral home, but it was all I needed.

So in September, I started school. I was the youngest guy in the class; most were military veterans. But I made friends quickly. There were a few with situations similar to mine. I made it through the probationary period and did all right on the entrance exams.

My best friend from school was Jeff. We hung together all the time. He lived in Monroeville, about forty-five minutes away. I would go there a lot on the weekends. About a month in, I got a full-time job at a local Pontiac dealer. So I was pretty busy during the week, thirty hours of school and forty hours at work. But on the weekends, it was party time. My buddy Jeff also had three sisters which made things more fun and interesting. Also, Jeff introduced me to all his local friends. So we always had things to do on the weekends. Sometimes we'd go camping and fishing. Sometimes we would go to a large cemetery where famous movies were made. We'd go after midnight when they were closed, take cases of beer, see if we could spook the ghosts, and raise the spirits. We had no success, but we had fun chasing the supernatural. We wanted to do what was wild and crazy accompanied by drugs and alcohol. Living in Pittsburgh was a very wild time of my life. Many bad things could have happened to me, but I had a guardian angel looking after me, undeservedly so.

I lived in McKeesport, just outside of Pittsburgh, for nearly two years. I had also bought a 1978 Honda 750 in my first year there. I would use it to go back to Toledo when the weather was good. At first, I'd go back every month or two; but as time went on, I'd go home less and less. I found there was plenty of excitement here. There was not a lot of police around, too many roads to cover. So I got comfortable with the steep inclines and winding roads, so I drove as fast as I could get away with. Most of the time, I was under the influence of something. God is the only reason I could have survived those two years. I did countless things that could have killed me or someone else or landed me in jail. I was always out to prove I was crazier and wilder than the next guy. I dated several girls while I was there, but my fun was more important. And when I was completed with school, I wanted no attachments. So through all this, I did finish school and received my airframe and power plant certificate, which meant I could legally work on all types of aircraft. After I graduated, I packed up all my stuff and headed back to Toledo. I thought, going back, I would get a good job and calm down a little.

So I came back to Toledo and moved back home for a while. Mom and Dad were easygoing and didn't try to enforce any rules on me. I met up again with my old friends and picked up right where I left off. After returning, I was sending résumés out and interviewing for jobs. I received an offer for a job in Cleveland as a helicopter minute man. I didn't know what that meant, but I turned it down. I said I didn't want to move again, and the money wasn't enough. But thinking back, I know that wasn't really the reason. I believe I was afraid to work on helicopters understanding my reality. I knew it would be a big risk to smoke weed, drink alcohol, and do the other things. I knew I couldn't live with that responsibility, but I still was unwilling to change my ways. I gave up what could have been a great career and settled for much less the entirety of my working career. Yet I was intelligent enough that I knew not to take that kind of risk. So I got a job as an auto mechanic and started working on getting certified. The money was good, and if I would make a mistake on a car, it would just get towed back in. The consequences could be much worse making mistakes on aircraft.

I loved riding my motorcycle every chance I had. I also had a few friends with motorcycles. We traveled around locally, raced, played, went to bars, and just had good times. But I was ready for some more adventure—I wanted to take a long trip. Well, my friends were all for it. So we all made a plan, the four of us, to go to Myrtle Beach the following summer. We vowed to save money and arrange it with our employment, and the date was set. During the time leading up, everyone was dead set on the trip. Even up until a week before our plan, we were all on board. I was so excited. I had saved money, completed maintenance on my motorcycle, and made arrangements with work. I was ready. Then just a couple of days before, my friends started dropping out one by one. They didn't really have a legitimate reason why; they just couldn't do it. I did not understand. We vowed, and now they were sliding out. I don't know if it was money, or if they were scared. I just couldn't believe all three were backing out. The night of departure, we were at our hangout spot; I was packed and ready. I spent hours pleading, trying to come up with solutions. Even my best friend, Joe, couldn't give me a reasonable excuse. I finally relented, realizing I was getting nowhere. I was very disappointed.

But I was also very determined and was not willing to change my mind and back out. So I left by myself. Traveling alone was not new to me, but I really wanted to share this adventure with my good friends. But at midnight, I hit the road; the weather was perfect. I rode all night but stopped for rest whenever I felt like it. The next morning, I was in Kentucky. Perfect weather again. I knew that I was on my own. I decided it was my trip—I went where I wanted, stopped when I wanted, and deviated from plans if I felt like it. Most states going south didn't have helmet laws. So I wore no helmet, just shorts, cowboy boots, no shirt, and just suntan lotion. I felt so free. I brought enough money to have a good time with no worries.

My motorcycle which had a king/queen seat, was a double sleeping bag behind me with tent on top. I sat on a down pillow with another pack on the fuel tank. I was packed well and quite comfortable. I figured out how to steer with my legs stretched out over the gas tank and with my feet resting on the front turn signals. If the pressure was from right foot on right-turn signal, I'd move left; and pressure on left, I'd move right. If I bent the throttle cable behind the tank bag, the throttle would stay. So I was able to fold my arms and steer with my feet. After a while, I got really good at this and comfortable. People really looked at me funny when I passed them, but it must've been a sight. So I was cruising like this through the Smoky Mountains over 100 miles per hour much of the time. The Honda 750 was smooth up to 115, and the mileage was amazing. Sometimes I would say to myself, "I'm getting off at the next exit no matter what and just go east to see where I end up." Traveling on my own, I didn't have to get approval or argue over changed destination. Now I was glad to be alone as I realized this was really the way I wanted it. Sometimes things just work out in my favor even if I didn't think so at the time. Needless to say, this ended up being the best trip I had ever enjoyed. The weather for the entire trip was awesome except for a couple of tropical rainstorms which just cooled me down. So I did go to Myrtle Beach, but I didn't stay. I decided to go to Florida and visit my friend Mark. Mark lived in Fort Lauderdale, and I hadn't seen him in a few years. Mark's family moved to Florida when Mark graduated from high school to take over a family business. So our friendship goes back to the fourth grade. When I met Mark, he punched me in the nose and gave me a bloody nose. I probably said something that offended him, and I was good at that. But after that, Mark felt bad, and we became good friends and partners in many capers. Mark is my best friend today, and we stay in touch.

But anyway, we had a great time in Florida. I stayed for a week. We went to Miami and went to every bar on the strip. Boy, what an experience that was. There were a few bumps in the road on the trip. I did get a speeding ticket, but only one. My lights went out at night in Daytona, and I had problems with my chain stretching. I had to adjust it a few times. But that just makes things interesting, I always welcome a little challenge. So the trip lasted two weeks, and I made it home safely. And of course, I had to rub it in to my friends and let them know what they missed out on. But after this, my friends lost some importance to me. I learned not to depend on friends. Have fun with them, but be careful whom you trust. So I did learn some valuable life lessons that have stuck with me until today. I've learned to set my own destination and not rely on anyone, except the direction and will of God.

So after I returned, I got back to my old routine. I did get a different job, but my bar life increased. I would travel around to the biggest clubs I could find and was drinking hard liquor. Then one Friday night, I was coming home on the expressway after drinking several double shots of 151 rum. What was I thinking? Ohio state troopers pulled me over and tested me. I had no business driving, but I was anyway. So I went to jail, and my car was left sitting along the expressway for the night. This was the second time I spent the night in jail, and I didn't like it, especially drunk and hungover. So now I had my first DUI. So after going to court, because of other points against me, I lost my license for a year. What a blow. My employer let me go because I couldn't test-drive customer cars. My employer did allow me to collect unemployment, so at least I had income for a while. So I temporarily moved in with my brother, Ben, in his apartment while I got my life back in order a little. You would think I would cut down on drinking, but it didn't affect me. Now I didn't have to worry about driving. I was in walking distance of my favorite bar. A friend of mine hired me for part-time mechanical work and would pick me up sometimes. But it still was very difficult not having freedom to travel as I please. So as my year suspension was getting close, I purchased a 1970 Chrysler New Yorker from a mechanic friend from my previous job. So I was ready when the year was up. Well, the time was up, but still no license in the mail. Well, the impatient person I was, I started driving. Just necessity at first, getting to work, and just minimal driving. I was using license plates off my other car that was in storage, so I was careful not to break laws. But after a few weeks of nothing in the mail yet, I got comfortable driving everywhere.

The story I am about to tell, again, God spared my life but did much more. God saved me from my own stupidity and spared other people's lives that I could have killed that day. Christmas Day could have easily put me in prison for life or have had me killed. I may have had to spend the rest of my life with someone else's death or maimed for life because of my selfish, reckless, and stupid actions that could've changed the course of mine and others' lives.

Christmas Day, 1981, I was driving on Benore Road when I saw one of my old friends spinning donuts in an empty parking lot. I was driving with my friend Joe, and we were having just a couple of beers, not drunk but charged up. When I saw our other friend spinning donuts, the wildness in me came to life. So I punched the pedal to the metal. The old Chrysler, maintained by a good mechanic, took off like a rocket. Just as I pushed past 90 miles per hour, there was a cop coming toward me from the other direction with his radar on. Sure enough, he turned on his lights, made a U-turn, and started after me.

(Author Note)

In the previous paragraph, I refer police as cop; this was our language of the day and probably worse, but the police never dished out to me more than I deserved and most of the time I got off easy. Out of respect for police and law enforcement, I will not use the word cop for the remainder of the book yet will be honest about the events that had transpired my thoughts and prayers go out to the families that have lost their loved ones in the line of duty. I honor the police for the sacrifice they make for our freedom and safety.

I told Joe, "I can't stop, or we'd be caught. Gotta go. Joe, get rid of beer bottles."

So he worked on that, and I drove. What was I thinking? What a stupid idea. So Joe was getting rid of empty bottles, and we were flying to avoid the consequences of the law. We headed up over an overpass. At the bottom of the hill was Suder, and we needed to go right. Luckily, it was clear. We hit the turn at a high rate of speed with all four tires squealing. After that, another intersection and a fast left turn. Now, we were heading into a residential area, and the police cruiser was not to be seen. So I headed up a side street. The coast looked clear. So I decided to head up Summit Street and go into Michigan. Lots of back roads to lose them for good. But as soon as we turned onto Summit, there were Toledo police coming at us from both directions. Coming up to Summit was my mistake. We should've abandoned the car in the neighborhood and reported it stolen. That's what I told myself after the fact; but even if I had gotten away, eventually, I was destined to be caught. So we hit the side streets again, and now there was local traffic. I didn't care. I wove in and out passing cars like they were sitting still. Every time I'd turn, there would be another police cruiser I could outrun their cars but not their radios. Now I could understand why I had heard that said in the past. Finally, we were cornered by about six police cruisers. So I stopped, got out, and put my hands up. Time to face the music. All the policeman were very angry for good reason—Christmas Day, so senseless. They were pushing me, yelling at me, calling me names, and kicking my legs. They were trying to get me to resist for cause to beat me up. But spectators were all around now, so they had to calm down some.

So they cuffed me, then they all sat there writing tickets. I had no warrants and no real record other than a suspended license, but they handed me over to the one who started the chase to take me downtown. So I was locked up again for a few hours. Then my girl-friend at the time came and picked me up. So they let me out with a court date pending. We went from there to my family get-together where I told everyone about my day. Now they must've all thought I was really crazy; I did. But I figured they would all find out any-way, so no reason to try to hide it. But I didn't have that girlfriend much longer, but that wasn't unusual. For me, most girls don't want a guy who's always getting in trouble and not able to drive. Besides that, drinking, partying, and being with my friends was what I was most interested in. Boy, I sure got myself into a mess this time. I had a stack of tickets three-quarters of an inch thick. Every policeman there wrote me as many as they could. And hey, I deserved them all. The transmission in my Chrysler was fried, so I sold it as is for what-ever I could get. Driving was over; and now I needed all I could get for a lawyer, fines, and court costs. But still it could've been a whole lot worse. So I found a lawyer who was a friend of my family and good guy who would do the best he could and be fair with me. So I visited my new lawyer; and he said I could do possible jail time, lots of cost, and not drive for a long time.

So this kind of settled my wildness for a while, awaiting a call from my lawyer. Meanwhile, I worked all I could saving as much money as possible.

Then finally, the call came.

Jim, my lawyer, said, "I have good news, and I have bad news. What do you want first?"

I hesitated a little, then said, "The bad."

"Guess what, your fee has just been doubled."

I said, "What? What's wrong?"

And he responded, "The judge just happens to owe me a favor, and your license will be reinstated."

Hardly believing what I just heard, I said, "Sure, no problem."

Now he didn't tell me what kind of favor the judge owed him, but that was irrelevant. I couldn't believe my ears.

But he said, "You do have to appear in court and be sentenced and fined."

So I wasn't out of the woods yet, but it looked a whole lot better than what I had been expecting. So after a few weeks, I appeared in court with Jim. Now remember that my 1970 Chrysler had license plates from my 1970 Ford Thunderbird on it. So the judge was reviewing my charges and started out with a joke.

He said, "I see you were driving a 1970 Ford. Well, you were fighting a losing battle from the start."

Then he started laughing, he believed, at my expense. But I stayed very quiet, was careful not to smile, and let him have his laugh. But I chuckled to myself knowing I had been driving a 1970 Chrysler.

Then he said with a serious look, "I'm giving you a break you don't deserve. I better not see you back in this courtroom for as much as spitting on the sidewalk, or I will lock you up, and you won't drive again for a long, long time."

So I told the judge I was sorry and thanked him, and it was over. I paid my fines and paid my lawyer, and three months after the escapade, I was driving legal again. Only one of the officers showed up to court; so all other charges had been dropped if I pleaded guilty to excessive speed, reckless operation, and eluding, which I did. They never caught me on the wrong plates. I guess that was just too insignificant. I had been clocked at 108 miles per hour in a 25-miles-per-hour zone. God had interceded for me again. It was the only thing that could explain this sequence of circumstances.

What the judge and Jim, my lawyer, told me, I took to heart. I did not get another ticket or any trouble with the law for a long time after that. I drove very cautious, obeyed the laws, and drank at home. I was still wild but a little smarter about it. I got another auto mechanic job. It wasn't big money. But I liked it, and I liked the owner. The owner, Frank, was an older mechanic. He taught me a lot and gave me the freedom to work on anything, including my own cars on the weekends.

CHAPTER 3

Destructive Cycles

TO THE READER, I'D like to offer some insight into my purpose for writing this book. These designated principles are very important to me because I lived these experiences and now am experiencing a new life, a second chance, and I want to help others who want to find a better life. First, I hope your reading will be hopeful, interesting, intriguing, encouraging, enlightening, and inspiring. Two, the importance to recognize how the powerful progression of drugs and alcohol can change the way of rational thinking. Three is hope. It is powerful, it is life changing, it is essential to recovery, it is uplifting, it is attainable, it is possible for anyone, it brings a future of happiness and fulfillment, it brings selflessness, and it brings prosperity. It comes from God.

In the beginning, drugs and alcohol were a lot of fun for me, but the problem is that it doesn't last. The fun and happiness is superficial, and after some time, that ended. And when that happened, I was stuck with a smorgasbord of addictions which I could not stop on my own power. When I was young, I didn't think that could ever happen to me. So I became reckless, and it progressed, dragging me down slowly. I fought the good fight, but it took me down to rock bottom.

So the main purpose of this book is to instill hope; that is where true recovery begins.

So on with my story. Life was looking up. My job fixing cars was challenging. We did all kinds of repairs, and I was learning a lot. I had my drivers license, and I was renting a house from my brother-in-law, Tom, and my sister, Sunny, and it was a really nice house with a garage and two of my friends shared the rent. We partied at the house, so I didn't drive needlessly. For extra money, I would buy cars, fix them, and resell them. It was fun because I would drive them until they sold, so I was able to drive different cars. I had a coworker named Bob. We got to be pretty good friends working together. One day, Bob offered me a deal on a car he wanted to sell. It was a 1974 Javelin. He said all it needed was an engine, and he would sell it for $100. It looked good, couple of dings but no rust. So I bought it. So I went shopping at the cheapest junkyard I knew of.

He said, "Yeah, no problem. Go pick one. I can sell it for one hundred dollars. If it's bad, I'll give you another one."

I said, "Can't I hear one run?"

He told me, "We don't have any you can see run, but you have thirty days to return it if you're not happy."

Wow, that was kinda risky, but $100 is reasonable. So I found one in the Gremlin with 56,000 miles and 304 cubic inches. When they pulled it, they dragged it over six cars to get it out. I was very discouraged. They beat it all up, but I took it and hoped for the best. I did a lot of work to replace the bent and dented parts. Then I installed it into the Javelin, and it started right up. Boy, was I thrilled when I drove it. What a great running engine, and it was fast.

So after a couple of weeks of cleaning the car up and fixing minor things, I placed an ad in the Blade for sale. After several calls on it, one day, an older lady showed up at the shop in a big Oldsmobile to look at the car. The lady looked wealthy and well dressed—classy lady—and spoke very professionally. She was obviously very intelligent. She wasn't interested in driving the car. Instead she persuaded me to drive the car to her apartment and show it to her granddaughter. This lady was very smooth, but for some reason, I trusted her. It was probably a thirty-mile drive to her apartment. Well, the idea kind of intrigued me. I figured what the heck. When I got there, the granddaughter didn't seem too thrilled, but she followed her grandmother's suggestions. So we went for a drive; she drove, hardly saying two words. Then we returned. Grandma invited me in for coffee. There was nothing really wrong with the car, so that wasn't in question. Then the negotiations started. She talked me into payments. That's not what I was looking for because I knew people couldn't be trusted. But I made the deal. She gave me a down payment, and I believed she would keep her word. I would need to go back to give her the title; and Lisa, the granddaughter, would make payments from her waitress income. Lisa was a hard worker and a person true to her word also. When I went back for my next visit, Grandma talked us into going out after we were done. Lisa was hesitant, but she finally agreed. So we went out, and we had a great time and hit it off right from the start.

So I started visiting Lisa and Grandma a lot. Grandma and I would have long conversations. She knew a lot about business, and that really interested me. So we got along great. She encouraged Lisa and me to spend time together, and we did. Lisa did not want to owe me, so she paid off the car much sooner than we agreed. She liked it pretty well.

Now, before I met Lisa, I was still headed down a dead-end road. I was getting reckless and careless again and wiped out my motorcycle three times. Since I was living with two other guys, there was a party at the house every night. We had a pool table in the living room, and we played a lot of cards. Other than working, drinking, and having parties every night, my life was going nowhere. I was involved very little with my family except for Ben because they lived a different lifestyle. When I met Lisa, I was ready to start settling down some, and my life was depending on it. Lisa and I fell in love very quickly and decided to get married. I was twenty-two, and she was nineteen—both still quite young. But after three months together, we planned our wedding. At first, we were just going to go to the justice of the peace. Now my brother Bob, my oldest brother and very wise, helped persuade me to have a small church wedding. Of course at this time, I didn't want anything to do with church. So hesitantly, we both agreed and found a United Methodist pastor willing to marry us. Grandma was very disappointed with this idea. She wanted us to have a Catholic wedding and offered to pay for it if we could wait six months. But we didn't want to wait, so we stuck with our plan. So Joe was my best man; and Mareen, Lisa's best friend, was her maid of honor. We left the wedding with a procession of motorcycles. The motorcycles were decorated and had strings of beer cans tied behind them. So we all paraded around, then we went down to the riverside and toasted a bottle of champagne. So my friends had to move from the house now that I was married. I was ready for them to move. Things were out of hand. So we spent our first night at home and packed for our honeymoon using my motorcycle.

As we left Toledo, it was cloudy but not raining yet. Now we really didn't plan for rain going down. I thought it would be smooth sailing just like when I had traveled down there alone. By the time we traveled an hour, the rain began. So we stopped, thinking we could wait it out. But after a while, it didn't stop, so we got moving again. When we got to a town, we bought some cheap rainsuits. They didn't last long; they ripped to shreds. So we traveled through Ohio all rain; we were soaked. As we entered Kentucky, rain was tapering off a little. I was following close behind a truck going eighty, not realizing that Lisa was almost falling off the back. Finally she let me know she needed to stop. So I rolled off I-75 and stopped along a ditch. Lisa was sick and throwing up. So we decided it would be a good time to find a motel. I imagined Lisa was wondering what the heck she had gotten herself into.

This was just the beginning of some tough times coming for Lisa, not just this trip. Anyway, we found a nice motel for our first honeymoon night. Lisa was sicker than a dog crying for her mother. But she was stuck with me. I stayed up with a six-pack, watching movies all night. In the morning, Lisa was a little better, so we went and had a good breakfast, then hit the road again. It wasn't any better, and it rained all the way to Myrtle Beach. But we made it. The rain stopped, and it was beautiful at the beach. We stayed a couple of days enjoying the weather and our honeymoon before our trip home. On the back of our motorcycle was a "Just Married" sign we carried the entire trip. People would honk and wave, and we liked that not many couples take their honeymoon on a motorcycle. So then we headed back home, and it didn't rain, not one bit. The trip home was hot, blistering sun. We both were sunburnt and blistered, hoping it would rain, but it didn't. From one extreme to another, there were no mishaps on the ride, but we were both glad to get back home. We both had our fill of riding for a while. It put our new marriage to the test also, but we made it and stayed together after.

After we were home for a while, my brother Ben, who worked at Jeep, told me they were hiring and needed mechanics. Now I had received all my automotive certifications over the last couple years, so I decided I'd go apply at Jeep. So I showed up at the Jeep employment office. I asked them if they were taking applications. They told me no and that I would have to go through the employment service.

Then I said, "I was told you were looking to hire certified auto mechanics."

The man instantly changes his tune.

He said, "Oh, you are a certified mechanic. Come in. Let's talk."

Well, they hired me on the spot and wanted me there 8:00 a.m. the next morning. I told them I needed to give notice to my boss.

He said, "If you want the job, start tomorrow or else not."

When I told my boss, he was really upset. I told my coworker, then he went over and applied too. They did the same thing to him, and he started the day after I did. Now we were the only two mechanics at this shop. We both didn't like leaving like that, but the opportunity just couldn't be passed up. We were both working mandatory seventy hours a week for the first six months, and we worked more than seventy. I liked the overtime; it was more money than I had ever made in my life.

So now I was in the big-time, so next we moved to a big old house mainly because it had a four-car garage. So I was making this good money but spending it and depending on the overtime. It didn't do a lot for a new marriage, and we fought quite a bit. She didn't like being home alone a lot, and when I wasn't working, I was drinking with my friends. So what should have been a great beginning was kind of rocky. We had plenty of extra space; so David, Lisa's younger brother, moved in with us for a while. So I thought that might help her; she was close to David. The company would help her as for me being gone a lot.

Well, the good times at Jeep didn't last very long. They changed my shift, took away my mechanic job, and put me on the assembly line with less overtime. I started to hate my job. I wasn't cut out to work on an assembly line. I felt I was working in a prison, so the impulsive person I was, I just up and quit after ten months. And to top it off, Lisa was pregnant. I made no plans where to work, and I didn't have enough money saved for this kind of decision. Now we would have to move from this big house but had nowhere to go. So I decided to get a camper trailer, and we'd live in campgrounds for the summer. I was able to get a mechanic's job, but the money was about one-third of what I made at Jeep, but it would help us just get by until I could find a better job. During these times, I just didn't think things through. I was very impulsive and reckless and cared only about my selfish desires or my discomforts being remedied. So now we were homeless. I bought an old station wagon to pull our trailer around. Sometimes living in the campground was fun when our friends and family came to hang with us. Then one day, something terrible happened. Lisa was walking barefoot on the wet sand, and when she reached for the metal trailer door, electricity grabbed her arm and took control of her body. She was being bounced back and forth against the trailer side, not able to get away. Screaming, realizing no one was going to help her, she peeled her fingers from the doorknob one at a time with her other hand. She fell to the ground, heart racing and barely able to breathe. Shortly after, I found her crying, mascara running down her cheeks, fingers cut and bleeding, distraught, and terribly worried about our baby she was carrying. I did my best to calm and comfort her to no avail, and we went right to the hospital. This is what can happen if a two-prong cord is used instead of a three-prong. I didn't know this, and I had no idea this could happen. Her body became the path of electricity with her feet grounded to the wet sand. So at the hospital, they took x-rays and checked her and the baby's vitals. They could only know so much, they said. Everything looked okay, but Lisa was very worried and never stopped until Colette was born. After this episode, we realized we needed a safe environment and started looking for apartments. We had lived in several different places including staying on my family's vacant land for a bit. After three to four months of this, we needed a more adequate living situation. We finally got enough money together to move into an apartment in the late summer. We were very happy to move to an apartment by now. Shortly after moving, I was offered a good job. I accepted the job at a Toyota dealer as an auto technician—not quite as much money as Jeep but a good dealer with great perks and benefits. I still had all my certifications, so I started at top pay scale. By now, Lisa was just a few months from delivery. We were starting to get our lives in order, managed to furnish our apartment, and finally get a little comfortable.

January 1, 1985, Colette was born; she was small but healthy. I was there for delivery and cut the cord. It was a happy day. Life was starting to look better for us. We were able to pay our bills and get a little ahead. After living apartment life for a while, we decided a house was a better investment and a better environment to raise our daughter. We didn't have enough money for a down payment, so I asked my brother Bob if he could help us out. Bob was always willing to help when he could, so he loaned us enough to purchase our first home. It was a small two-bedroom that needed some work, but we were happy to have our own home. It had a shared driveway, small lot, and one-car garage with a full basement. After working at Toyota for two years, I became burnt out on flat-rate mechanics. So I quit and decided it was time to go into business for myself. But this time, I did have a plan. I would work carpentry part-time for my brother John and his wife Linda. John was a general contractor and always needed workers, and he was more than willing to teach me the trade. He was a housebuilder—doing additions, kitchens, bathrooms, and all aspects of remodeling, residential and commercial. I also started business in seal-coating asphalt driveways and parking lots and plowing snow in the winter. My business names were Sealy Sam and Sam's On Time Snow Removal. I did these two businesses for seven to eight years. They were tough, profitable when busy but a lot of lost time due to the weather. So when I wasn't seal-coating, I was doing carpentry for John. Also, I was a subcontractor for John, so there were no benefits. So after a couple of years, I needed to file for bankruptcy. We were able to keep our house and vehicles and able to shed unsecured debt.

So after bankruptcy, I started doing more versatile work, repairing cars and some home repair. I was making more for John because I had gained some experience. Our credit was damaged, so we were kind of stuck for a while. Lisa worked full-time as a dental assistant while also going through school. Then we got some news that my brother Bob's in-laws had a house they previously lived in it but moved, and they needed to sell it. They had tried through a realtor. But the house needed some things, and they weren't able to sell. So Wanda's mother, Sara, (Wanda is Bob's wife) called me and said she was willing to work out a deal. I did explain my situation to her about our finances, but she said that was okay. She knew I was working. She offered a deal I couldn't turn down—very little down, reasonable price, no interest, and land contract. This house was a two-story and had two-car garage, three bedrooms, and fenced backyard with our own concrete driveway. No brainer. Better neighborhood and bigger all the way around. Yeah, it needed work, but that's what I do. We knew we would have more kids, and this was much better to raise a family. So we made the deal and moved to our new home. We kept the other house, and it became our first rental property. So construction was my main source of income now. I still seal-coated and plowed snow as much as I could. I also still bought and sold cars and repaired cars. I worked all the time; I spent a lot of time in the sun. When I was home, I drank a lot of beer. I was depressed. Not enough excitement. So I needed to do something.

CHAPTER 4

Life Is about Risks

S O JOE AND I planned a voyage of Lake Erie. We planned this trip for several weeks. West Sister Island is about twenty-five miles across the western end of the lake. Lake Erie is not the deepest lake, but it can be treacherous. This lake can be very unpredictable; storms pop up fast and hard. But Joe and I grew up near Lake Erie, fishing and camping. We felt we were old veterans. I had never sunk a boat but had come close many times. So we were planning to stay there for two nights. I think we both had become nonchalant about the true dangers of Lake Erie and just believed we would always go through it like in the past. We used my boat, a sixteen-foot fiberglass hull with an old Mercury outboard. I had used it a couple of years, so it seemed to run pretty good. We brought everything we thought we had to have. We removed the Styrofoam flotation from under the deck to give more room for storage of provisions. We'd be gone for three days and two nights. We intended to be completely prepared. These provisions included twenty-two gallons of gas and a cooler packed with our favorite foods—steaks, eggs, bacon, sausage, and more. We also brought a car battery, television, and a cooler packed with high-quality beer. We were really gonna rough it with a TV. Needless to say, we were way overloaded and had removed the only flotation. But we had to have it all to make our voyage successful. So in the evening, we launched into the Ottawa River, taking our time at loading to be sure we had everything that we needed.

As far as we looked out onto the river, we noticed it very calm—no wind and the water looked like a sheet of glass. As we loaded, the sun was just going down, and the sky was clear. We both agreed it would be more fun and more exciting to travel through the night. Surprisingly, neither one of us thought anything could go wrong, just another boat ride and a good time.

So off we went. It was a beautiful night. As we headed out of the river into the bay, it became just a little choppy. As we passed the last parts of the mainland, we were into one- or two-foot waves. No problem. After about fifty minutes, as we were discussing our provisions, we realized we forgot worms. After a disappointing conversation, we agreed we had to go back to get them. So we returned, and when we made it back, we'd lost two hours. Then we noticed waves were bigger now, the sky cloudy, and the wind picking up. But we weren't gonna change now. The forecast had looked okay. We still thought the return for worms, although a waste of time, was necessary because I had been stranded on West Sister and we were unable to find worms or grubs; so we weren't going to be without good bait. Now the waves were two to four feet as we passed the outer light. Nothing could deter us from our destination now. We might get a little wet, but we'd build a huge fire and dry off once we arrive. So we just plowed along watching Johnny Carson and drinking a few beers.

It was about time to switch gas tanks, so I told Joe, "Hey, I'll slow down so you can go back and switch tanks. If we're idling, the engine tanks can be switched without killing the engine."

He agreed. I throttled back. Just then, the engine quit, and water rushed around our ankles. We knew in an instant we were in trouble. Apparently, we had been taking on more water than we thought. We had a bilge pump, and I knew it was working. But it really didn't matter. We had to think fast. So I attempted to restart. If it was running, we'd bail while moving. But I tried to restart. It was useless, and waves were sweeping over the transom. In seconds, the back end of the boat was going down. We now both realized that we were in peril.

I said, "Joe, grab your seat cushion."

Our life jackets were under the deck. There was no time to find them. Very soon, the front of the boat was up like a cork. Now we were just hanging on, hoping it would stay up. But we could hear air rushing out of an old eyelet hole in the front tip. The air hissed loudly, and we could hear the bilge pump running at full speed, and we could see the bow lights still on. It only took about one minute from the time water was rushing around our ankles, until we watched and listened as the boat disappeared.

Now the boat was gone. There was no one around, and we were treading water. The only things we had at this point were our seat cushions with straps. As the waves were sweeping over our heads, we could see debris from the boat floating. I grabbed a two-gallon gas can, and Joe grabbed two-quart oil containers. We both knew, to have any chance of survival, we needed to sober up quick and use our heads. We both put our legs into the straps of the cushions to ride them like a saddle. We needed to keep as much above the surface as possible to help prevent hypothermia. I needed to go underwater while I held the gas can over my head in order to empty it.

Joe started yelling, "Sam! Sam!"

When I finally came back up, Joe was really worried. He thought I was drowning.

I said, "I'm fine. Just emptying the gas out."

"Man, I thought you were going down."

Joe emptied the oil containers and put them in his shorts. It was probably 1:00–2:00 a.m. It was dark; the waves were about six feet. We didn't know how far land was, and nobody would be out this far this time of night. The only thing we could do was to keep moving, keep our bodies buoyant, stay calm, and stay alert. So we tried to stay together. We talked; we prayed. We were thinking we might not make it. I told Joe I just didn't believe that it was my time yet. We just kept going until morning and attempting to swim towards the island. We knew before the ship went down that we were going with the waves, so we continued in that direction. Neither one of us were very spiritual, but being in this predicament, we were asking God to save us from this one. Now isn't this so typical and so common while we are in peril. This is when we ask God's help. But we didn't know if God was listening to us. Neither one of us were deserving of God's grace. I sure wasn't; the only time I thought about God was when I was in trouble. Joe and I were both optimistic individuals, but we knew we were in a serious predicament we may not survive. It was a long night. We were tired and shivering.

Back at home, about the time the boat went down, Lisa was alerted too. She was awakened abruptly when the fan fell to the floor for no apparent reason. Immediately, Lisa knew that something was wrong. She was against the idea of a voyage in the first place. She knew it was a reckless idea. But she also knew I was stubborn and bullheaded and wouldn't change my mind. But she was very worried and felt the need to get up and pray for us. So knowing that something was wrong, she continued praying while we continued swimming. It was the only thing she could do. We didn't have cell phones yet, but we couldn't have answered even if we did. The water temperature we estimated to be sixty-five to sixty-eight degrees, cold enough for hyperthermia, so we were worried about that. I was wearing long pants and a flannel long-sleeve shirt. Joe only had shorts and a tank top. Now the gasoline that I drained on myself was mixed with oil and soaked into my shirt and was irritating my skin. Joe seemed to be colder than I, but he kept going. Joe and I had been best friends for a long time, so we talked about all kinds of things. That helped keep us going. Finally, daylight was on the horizon but no stars, no sun, foggy, and gloomy—but we were still alive and still treading water. As it got a little brighter, we could see the island. The island was still miles away, and the mainland, we couldn't see it at all. The current was heading north, so even swimming was hard. The current could carry us right past the island. But we didn't have a lot of choices, so we swam the best we could toward the island. By now, we were both shaking; hypothermia was probably setting in. But neither one of us was gonna give up until we were done. I was really worried about Joe. His skin was turning purple. I don't really know how I looked, but it probably wasn't good either. Even if we made it to the island, how would we build a fire? And there was no food or freshwater, and we tried not to drink the lake water. The island was so far off. We were both shaking uncontrollably. We both knew only a miracle could save us now, but we did our best to keep going. Then suddenly, through haze, we could see what appeared to be a boat. Could it really be, or were we seeing things? Who would be out here on a day like today? But as we looked, a blue-and-white boat was coming toward us. We both started yelling and waving the best we could with our diminished energy levels. Wow, were we really going to be rescued? The boat came directly to us; there were three men on board as they idled toward us; we could see three strange looking men like the kind of faces I'd never seen anyone even look similar to. When they got close enough to us, they helped us get on board. The men didn't say anything that I remember. They didn't ask questions like "What happened?" or "Why are you floating out here?" They pointed to the back of the boat where they wanted us to sit. I thought maybe they were deaf or couldn't speak. There was no visible fishing equipment on board, so why were they out there. We were glad to be out of the water; it didn't matter.

So they turned and headed toward the mainland. Going back, we sat getting splashed. We were still shaking uncontrollably. They never offered a blanket or to go into the cabin. They just stared at us and never said a word. Joe and I looked at each other. We knew this was very strange, but our prayer had been answered. We were so thankful to be going back to dry land. We told them what had happened to us, but they didn't respond. It seemed they already knew what happened and they were here to retrieve us, and that's all. Joe and I were shaking cold, exhausted, hungry, and thirsty; but we were alive.

We finally arrived at a marina gas dock with a small store. The men dropped us off, and when we looked out, they vanished just as quickly as they had appeared. Joe was on the ground, kissing the pavement and thanking God. I also thanked God, but I was cold and thirsty and headed into the store. The girl working the store was very helpful and understanding. She gave us free coffee and let me use the phone. When I called Lisa, she told me about her experience at home that night and headed out to pick us up.

Well, we had our adventure and excitement. For a while, we came very close to a watery death and lived to tell the story. We knew that we were rescued by angels of God. There was nothing coincidental about it. God didn't get the glory he deserved because I still was not ready to change my way of life. God did bless me with a greater faith and has been with me for many more experiences in my life where I cannot deny his presence.

Despite my reckless behavior, God sent his angels to rescue me. I did not deserve God's grace. But God protected me and my family. My daughter, Colette, would have grown up without a father. Lisa wouldn't have had the father to help raise Colette. Both my sons, Sam and Michael, unborn, would not have existed today. God blessed my family beyond whatever I deserved, and he continues to bless my family today.

When we returned home, I ate and went to bed and still shook and shivered for hours. I'd like to say that my life changed completely after that excursion, but it didn't. I was very thankful to be safe and alive, but I was still selfish and greedy and not ready to make any substantial changes in my life. I still always put myself first, and I could never get enough of what I thought made me happy.

CHAPTER 5

Building a Life

S O AFTER THE BOAT incident, I did calm down a little for a while. I told myself I'd never own a small boat again because that must've been the reason for nearly drowning. So I bought a twenty-five-foot cabin cruiser and rented a dock space, and life was good again. I took it out in all weather, but it plowed right through it. I still wasn't afraid of the lake, but I was a little smarter about it and made safety more important. And now we had cell phones, so communication was much better. I had fun with that for a while, then I sold it being bigger boat's incurr, bigger expences.

Then August 6, 1990, our first son, Sam, was born. I was there in delivery and cut the cord. We were both thrilled—now a boy and a girl. Life had improved for us in many ways but still not in what really counts. Drinking and excitement still dominated my life, and I worked seven days a week, chasing dreams. I owned several rental properties which kept me away much of the time. Lisa worked extra hard to take up the slack in my absence, and she still worked full-time also. We also remodeled our house—new roof, new facade on the front, jacked-up garage, and remodeled all rooms in the house including the basement. But after all of this, instead of being happy and content, I was depressed. Then construction slowed down, and working without health insurance was difficult. During this slow-down, my brother Dick offered me a job at his electric-motor shop. He needed me to work on standby generators and welders. It was a good job, full-time with good benefits, so I took the job.

Dick was a great employer and a great role model. Dick always put God first; no matter what, he would always leave early for his church obligations. Dick was driven; he was fearless when it came to big jobs, maybe even a little reckless with some things, but he was a stable, solid man of God, and I always admired that about him. Dick passed away November 27, 2020, and is missed by many.

I worked for Dick and his wife Barb for a couple of years and kept buying rentals during that time. I now owned one fourplex, three duplexes, and three houses; and I still planned on buying more. My monthly income was substantial, but I worked hard to sustain it. I collected all rents in person. I did all repairs, and I also did all evictions. That was a full-time job in itself. Then September 5, 1996, my second son was born. I was in delivery again and cut the cord. We really wanted our third to be a boy so Sammy would have a playmate. So our wish came true. My life was great, but I had a hard time rec-ognizing it. I was envious of people having new homes to raise their families. Why couldn't I have that too?

One day, Lisa said to me, "We can build. We have the means."

That was all I needed to get the gears going. So we decided the best way to do it was to sell our house and use the profit for a down payment. I had the experience now because I had built many homes working for John and was confident I could build our own. So we put our house on the market after staging it and preparing. Within a few months, we sold it and profited as good as we had hoped for. We had thirty days to move, so we had to get busy finding a lot and some place to stay. We took many long drives looking for lots. There were plenty of farmland lots, small lowlands, and areas we weren't thrilled with. One day, on our drive, we ended up in Elmore. What a nice little town. Elmore was on the Portage River, rocky with areas of rapids. This area had the kind of character we hoped for. So we fol-lowed River Road out of town a ways, and wouldn't you know, there were several lots on the river. When we first looked, we thought they would be out of our price range. But they were by owner and a phone number on the sign. I called, and the owner came right down to talk to us. I asked him how much. He said $30,000. I couldn't believe my ears. Three and one-half acres on the river, one acre of aged woodland, a stream bordering the lot, and a large hill in the front—so the house could be built into the hill. So being the negotiator I was, I offered him $28,000. He responded by laughing at my face.

I just smiled and said, "We will buy it. No problem."

The potential of this property was awesome. There was no end to what we could do with it. It was rough cultivated farmland—lots of poison ivy and rocks deep in weeds—but this would be our home. So we secured our financing, and using my brother John's name as licensed contractor, I'd be doing all the building. So I left my job with my brother Dick and would rely on rental income and proceeds from the home loan to pay bills while building. For eight months, my job was building the house. The only other work was collecting rent and doing emergency repairs. My brother-in-law Bret would help me when he could, but I was there every day.

I was very happy while building the house. Lisa and the kids were just as excited and helped as much as possible. It was a fulltime job. I pulled all permits, dealt with subcontractors and building inspectors, and ordered all materials and dealt with the bank. During this time, Lisa and I were staying in her mother's basement. The kids shared the upstairs bedrooms. Everyone was harmonious and understanding. It was a worthwhile sacrifice. It was not an easy winter to work through. We had a lot of rain, snow, and cold too. But nothing stopped me from moving forward. I also had better control over my drinking and was very dedicated to the job on hand. I loved every bit of the whole project. I was driven. I'd have a big fire at night and have some beers, but that was it. So for a time, my progression of drugs and alcohol slowed down. But it probably wouldn't last, and it didn't. But for now, it was a good time for the family. So in the spring, we moved into our new house. We still had a lot to do. Much of the house was done enough to satisfy the bank and the building departments. We worked the property for years—landscaping, planting trees, building a large garage, and adding another driveway, steps, and patios. It was never done, but that was how I planned it. But year after year, it became better and better with a lush lawn and beautiful trees, plants, and flowers. It was our dream home come to life. John and I even bought a lot across the street and built a house on specu-lation and listed and sold it. I started a business rehabbing rundown homes in Toledo. I worked as a contractor and was doing more than a dozen houses a year. I also bought a few more rentals. Now I was working seven days a week and was only home at night. From all the years of hard labor, I developed back issues, so I started taking pain pills. I started taking the pills with beer and became dependent on the combination. Then I bought a nine-unit apartment. I shouldn't have bought it. It was a money pit, and it only increased my work-load. So I could never catch up on work, and I was hiring out as much as possible to still be profitable. About this time is when banks were loaning as much as 125 percent of appraised value. Borrowing became very easy, so I took full advantage. I refinanced all the rent-als for close to 100 percent of value. One appraiser called me on an appraisal and asked me what number I was looking for. I told him what I wanted, and he said okay. He didn't even inspect the property. So I borrowed what I could, invested the best I could, but lived as well as I could also. For a while, it seemed like it would always be that way, but the bubble was going to burst. Still, I wasn't satisfied. I was always looking for more and beginning to lose rationale. I knew, in the back of my head, things weren't right. I just didn't understand what really lacked in my life, but I kept searching.

Members of my family attempted to reach out to me and give me answers. But truth was that drugs and alcohol dominated me, and I was not willing to give them up. I believed I needed them to get through my long, hard weeks, which I designed. I did believe in God, but I thought I could live the way I chose and still have a relation-ship. But it just didn't work. Even though I didn't follow God's will, he still continued to bless me and my family, but there were lessons on the horizon that I needed to learn. So I would go to church with the family sometimes and try to fit in, but I didn't. I would read the Bible for a period of time very intently and pray, but I didn't seem to get the answers I wanted. I wanted God to fix my problems, yet I didn't want to follow his will. So I did continue to seek God and was intrigued by spiritual people. I couldn't understand how people—without drugs, alcohol, excessive money, and little need for material things—could be so happy. And also these people are unselfish and wish to give their time to help people and their communities. These people are calm, relaxed, and content with whatever life dishes out. I would think, if I only had enough money and time so I wouldn't have to work so hard, then I'd have made it and be happy. But when I ask myself, Would that reduce my dependency? I have to say no. Nevertheless, I searched for a long time, much longer than I should have.

It was during these times that I experienced another monumental miracle that I still remember on a weekly and daily basis. From all the years of back-breaking work with carpentry, remodeling, and mechanics, I developed unrepairable back issues. Also from the accident as a child, my left leg was more than one inch shorter than my right. I had a terrible limp, and it was instrumental at putting my back out of line. Even though my relationship with God wasn't very good, I was always seeking him and interested at seeing him work. Self-medication was my remedy for pain and also for selfish comfort. I did have pain, but it was also an excuse when in excess. I read the Bible through a couple of times, but I used what I wanted and ignored the rest. God was always working in me and using other people to speak to me.

I was invited to my niece's wedding. I don't miss wedding invitations especially family. It was a Christian wedding, and almost all of my family were there. During the wedding, the bridegroom's guest speaker's name was Steve. Steve had a very interesting and intriguing message. Steve claimed that, through Jesus, he was blessed with the privilege to perform miracle healing. He proceeded to explain several miracles performed. Now this really interested me. I had a great faith due to my boat incident. I knew God is out there, but I had no ability to know his presence yet.

So after the wedding, everyone went to the reception hall. I couldn't stop thinking about Steve and the things he said. So I watched and waited until people were almost done eating and waited for an opportunity to approach Steve. When I saw him go for refreshment, I approached him and introduced myself. Steve was a very likable guy, and we had a great conversation. He was a very spiritual man, and I could feel it in his presence. After a little while, I told him about my physical problems. Of course, I didn't tell him about my addictions and my sinful nature. But he didn't pry and didn't seem judgmental in the least. Then he told me to sit in a chair and pull up my pant legs so he could see my legs. When I stretched them out, he could see clearly the difference in length. Then he put his hands around my left ankle and told me, when he said one word, my leg would grow. He then prayed a short prayer to God in Jesus's name, then said, "Jesus," and to my astonishment, I watched as my leg grew to the same length as the right leg. Recently, I had a physical with my doctor, and he remarked, "Normally, with this traumatic of an injury, one leg will be shorter than the other." I didn't say anything but inside I knew why. Well, I was amazed. I had never seen anything like this before. When I was picked up by God's angels off Lake Erie, I could say "Well, maybe, there just happened to be three guys in a boat that day." But I did know that there was much more to it than that. So I did believe what I had just experienced, and I was ecstatic.

Then he said, "Let's see about your back."

Then he put his arms around my waist and prayed, but I didn't feel anything. He told me that it wasn't God's will. He didn't have an answer as to why God didn't heal my back then. But I was still on cloud nine. Steve and I talked until most of the people had cleared out. He said that he attended a church where many were prophets and prophetesses. This reinforced my faith and helped make me more aware of God. I still prayed and read the Bible. I tried to live a moral life and do the right things. But I was not about to give up drugs and drinking. I also was still selfish and materialistic. Everything was about making money, having things, and becoming rich. Today I take no drugs and drink no alcohol, yet my back doesn't hurt. I am able to work hard all week. The doctor's diagnosis nearly twenty years ago was not good. So wasn't I healed that day, or was I? God can do things at his pace; giving my back instant healing that day wasn't his will. If he had healed my back, I probably wouldn't have changed my lifestyle. I needed to complete my journey, but I didn't know what it was yet. God had and has a plan for me, but it is entirely his choosing. God knew what was best for me and stayed with me and protected me through the journey. After time, this memory was clouded over by my life habits. I knew it was all real but still put it in the back of my mind. I never understood how the Israelites could sin after all the miracles they had witnessed. But I do now because the same thing happened to me, and God knew it would happen too. I couldn't understand how the same people that witnessed Jesus Christ's miracles crucified Him. Human nature along with Satan is a powerful force. I believe that miracles happen every day all around us, but we choose to call it Mother Nature or coincidence. I am no better. I still sinned; my life wasn't changed yet. After that wedding, I never saw Steve again, but I thank God for that spiritual and faith-building experience. Where I'm at today, I know God gave me more healing than I'm even aware of today. The reason I say this is because of much bigger things that happened after that day, later in life.

CHAPTER 6

The Fall

A FTER MY NIECE'S WEDDING, I was spiritually rejuvenated for quite some time. But my drug and alcohol use still kept increasing. Really, the only thing that remained was my faith, but I didn't know what to do with it. I read the Bible often, but I couldn't make any real changes for the real problems. Now Lisa worked full-time as a dental hygienist, and I was doing good rehabbing properties and still doing construction. So I decided it was time to get out of the rental business. This was about the time that real estate was becoming very volatile. The bubble was about to burst. Banks had been lending more than properties were worth, and delinquency rates were rapidly increasing. Now I had borrowed as much as I could get out of my rentals; so I knew I wasn't going to make much, if any, profit upon sales. But I started listing the more marketable ones and worked on the others. I sold one duplex and made $5,000. So I decided to auction three properties at one auction and to sell them one way or the other. I was able to sell all three, profiting $50,000 on two and losing $20,000 on the fourplex. But I was happy to be out from underneath. Shortly after this, my rehab company was shut down. This company was 75 percent of my income. I relied on them and had been working for them for about five years. This was a major blow. I was used to making big money. A regular job wouldn't do, and I had borrowed a lot of money against our home. I still needed to be rid of the rentals and continued to attempt selling. I tried to get out clean, but in the end, I failed.

My empire was crumbling, and I turned to alcohol for solace. This was a very hard time for Lisa and the kids, and I wasn't taking it well either. How humiliating this must've been. We were delinquent on the house payment, and my borrowing power was all used up. Then my one-year-old Dodge Ram diesel was repossessed and towed from our driveway. We didn't know how long before the bank would foreclose. We had lived here nearly ten years, and it was our home. We were at a loss what to do. We filed bankruptcy now for the second time, but that wouldn't solve all our problems. Our country was in a bad time now with financial institutions collapsing. Enron was the big news of the time. I had been swept up like many other property owners, and now was the time to pay the price. I had been reckless with the way I invested, hoping real estate value would keep increasing. Colette was in college at this time, so she wasn't as much affected. But Sam and Michael were in high school. Sam and Michael never complained. They went along with whatever we had to do. Why Lisa stuck with me with all the crap I put her through, I don't understand, yet there was much more to come. After losing our home, my business, and my truck, I had no motivation. I was just going through the motions out of obligation. I had to do what I could to keep my family. So I went to my sister Sunny and her husband, Tom, and told them about our situation. We decided to move back to Toledo and rent a house. Sunny and Tom loaned us the money for the deposit. Tom and Sunny helped us many times through the years and are great mentors. The house was okay, but nothing compared to where we came from.

So we moved. Sammy we put into Toledo Christian School, which he wanted, and Michael to Whitmer. The boys were okay with their school situation, and that we were thankful for. I got a job for a car dealer, fixing repossessed cars, kind of fitting for me. But I was an okay mechanic, and it paid the bills along with Lisa still working full-time. So we were getting by, but I was depressed and very unhappy with how things turned out. I would like to say that this was when I straightened my life out, but that was not how it went. I felt I had worked seven days a week all those years, all those rentals, and nothing to show for it. This was when I started buying lottery tickets. I decided this was how I would get rich again. I decided I wouldn't do it the traditional way. Work, save, invest. I would do it the quick easy way. But I needed to work to buy the tickets. I started small. But I studied the numbers and worked at beating the system, and I kept it to myself.

After we had lived in the rental house a short time, we had a big rain, and the basement flooded. We had a lot of our personal belongings stored in the basement and much of it was destroyed. So after cleaning up and throwing out many items that were personal to us, we were discouraged living in that house and wanted to move. About one year from the first house, another became available. My brother John owned a house next door to where I grew up, and he would rent it to us—a small house but more private and quite a bit cheaper. It needed work, but we could fix it the way we liked it. It was nothing special, but we all were more comfortable there. My parents' house was next door, and my mom was aging and needed help. My dad had passed away, and Mom was living on her own. But nothing had changed for me. I just existed and was very unhappy about life. I worked hard so I could still have as much as possible, and we fixed the house and made it our home. The kids were busy with sports and friends, so they moved on with their lives. A year after moving there, I quit the mechanic job and did whatever to get by with no real plan. Then I bought a boat from my sister-in-law. It was real cheap, and she let me make payments. A twenty-foot with inboard/outboard, it needed work, but it gave me a project. I did remodeling and started selling scrap in between. It kept me going with enough money to do what I wanted. I counted on Lisa to take up the slack. She always worked hard and stayed at her job. Lisa always paid the bills and worked hard to rebuild her credit. I didn't care a whole lot. I just drifted along for years, just looking for ways to make a fast buck but no real plan. We just continued to rent, and I couldn't get past the day-to-day. Then, because of a recommendation from a family member I was asked interview for a good job. So I went and interviewed and was offered a job as assistant plant manager for night shift. They hired me, and it was a wonderful opportunity. I had full benefits, and the pay was pretty good.

So things were looking up for us. It was a good job with a lot of responsibility. I started out taking it seriously. They drug tested, so I stopped smoking weed. I liked the job, and I had a lot of trust and freedom. We made cleaning products, and it was a growing, successful company. I had some connections that helped me out. So I was able to buy a nice car, and I had a dock space for my boat. But we still didn't own a home. This is when I started getting more serious about lottery tickets and was buying daily. I had a few wins, and that just motivated me all the more. My responsibilities included being on my feet most of the time which led to leg and back pain. So I asked my doctor to give me something strong for the pain so he prescribed me Vicodin. So now I would be able to pass drugs screens. That started out okay for a short while until I needed the effect of washing them down with beer. With this job and a decent car, I was starting to gain a little respect back, but I always seemed to sabotage my own success. Here I had a great job. I had keys to the plant. I ran the whole operation when the manager was on vacation. Who knows where it could have led? I worked along with the line workers and kept things running smooth. I had good health insurance and other benefits. I got along good with the bosses. I could have stayed there until retirement and done pretty well. But I still wasn't satisfied and took it for granted. I had enough money to be irresponsible again. It was summer. I worked nights, so I had daytime hours to play. While family was at work and school, I would go boating. While I was boating, I drank beer and started going to work feeling good. People at work were noticing the smell of alcohol. My manager talked to me and told me he was getting complaints. He said he understood, but I needed to cool it. I tried to cut down, and I thought I was hiding it better. One night coming to work, I was so lit that I called in sick. But on another night, management came to me and said I was to be tested. Well, of course, I didn't do well; and I was walked out of the plant that same night. Two years, I had worked there and now another great job becomes history because I couldn't control my drinking. The truth was that I couldn't stop but didn't really know it. Plus I didn't want to stop because I thought it was part of me. I didn't think I could ever be happy or fulfilled without drugs and alcohol. But this was still a big blow mentally and psychologically. I knew I was a loser, and I couldn't change that. Surprisingly, Lisa and the kids didn't seem that shocked. Nobody really said much; they could probably have easily predicted what was coming. Over the years, they could see the cycles I went through, but I couldn't, or I was just in denial. Well I was very remorseful and knew I needed to make a change.

So I did. I stopped drinking and started going to AA meetings regularly. So I managed to stop drinking, but I kept taking pills, saying that I needed them for pain. I never did smoke weed again. I figured, two years without, I didn't need it anymore. So I didn't drink, but I didn't follow the AA twelve-step program. I went every week, but more to keep Lisa happy. But I wasn't happy. I went along, but my life was miserable. But work was good. I had remodeling projects going all the time, and I collected scrap. I bought lottery tickets two times a day. When I won money, I kept it to myself. I actually did good sometimes. I was always hoping to make it big and show everyone how successful I was. I still just didn't get it, and I seemed to be clueless. Now I was over fifty years old. I believed it was too late for a new start. I blew every good opportunity I'd ever had; my only chance was to win it big with the lottery. I studied the numbers every day and thought I had a system. It was only a matter of time. And you know that's probably true, but how much time? And if God doesn't allow it, it may never happen. But I really believed it would and invested all I could manage but kept it hidden from everyone.

And not drinking was difficult every day, so I started drinking nonalcoholic beer. But I tried every brand until I found one that tasted the strongest.

So I started drinking a lot of nonalcoholic beer and would buy it by the case. It had a small amount of alcohol in it, but I figured that was okay. So I would wash down my pain pills with it and drink several so I could feel a little better. So after two years of not drinking real beer, I hadn't changed one bit. I was just replacing one addiction with another. And I didn't think I was being treated differently from my wife because I wasn't any different. The only difference was that I wasn't intoxicated, but I was still an addict. So I was grumpy, depressed, selfish, greedy, and unhappy. Sure, I was sober, but I was a dry drunk. But I didn't know it and wouldn't take the needed steps to correct it. Many things happened in the next few years; many things I just can't talk about to anyone, probably never. These were dark times in my life, about to get even darker.

Then Lisa planned a trip to go visit a friend for a week and asked me to take her to the airport. Sure, I said. I always enjoyed driving anywhere. But I also had my own little plan. I hadn't drunk real beer in over two years and had decided, while she was gone, I would enjoy myself. I had romanticized beer long enough I believed I could do it while she was gone and then stop again. So I dropped her off in Detroit at the airport and then looked for the nearest beer carryout.

CHAPTER 7

Decline

S O I LEFT THE airport, found the nearest carryout, and picked up a six-pack of the strongest beer I could find and as soon as I returned to the car, I cracked the lid and washed down a pill. Boy, was that first beer good...second and so on. When I got home, I bought more beer and kept drinking. What had I been missing? Why did I stop? Over two years of not drinking, and life was no better. Lisa didn't treat me any different; nobody did. Now I don't know if this was really true, but I believed it was.

So before I picked up Lisa at the airport, I got rid of all the evidence and pretended that everything was still okay. We went home, and everything seemed normal. But when we went to work on Monday, as soon as I got in my truck, I opened a beer and washed down a pill. It didn't take very long before Lisa found out I was drinking again. By now, I was not going to change.

I just told her, "Life hasn't changed, so I'm gonna drink, but I'll be controlled."

There wasn't much she could do at this point but accept it, but she was not happy about it and where it would lead to.

After this, I slowly rolled downhill. I finally sold my boat and then sold everything I could unload. I kept remodeling and also spent a lot of time hunting for and selling scrap, and now I just didn't care anymore. I am what I am, and it was just too late to change. I didn't want to change.

So I would start drinking when I left the house in the morning. It was harder to hide from people I was in contact with. I could tell by expressions on customers' faces that they smelled alcohol. But I still managed to do jobs. Then I spent the rest of my time collecting scrap. I would spend all scrap income on lottery tickets. When I'd win some money, I would double up on investments. But I took care of drugs and alcohol needs first. Also, during this time, I wasn't taking care of myself and developed dental problems. My front tooth broke off on an angle. It looked terrible and was uncomfortable eating. Also other teeth were breaking or needing work. This only made me more isolated, and Lisa told me it was caused by alcohol and opioids. I knew she was right, but I wouldn't admit it or change. Lisa is a licensed hygienist with many years of working experience and had seen this many times before. So I felt alone and didn't want to face people. This was all a bad combination. I would spend days scrapping and buying lotto tickets. I would have winning sprees, sometimes more than $15,000 in one month. But I didn't know how to handle it. I'd just spend more money on tickets and I'd feel good for a little while with a wad of cash in my pocket. I would pay some bills and do car repairs or what I could.

Then something good happened. I inherited a little money from the sale of my parents' home. I split it with Lisa so I could get my teeth fixed. Lisa took the other half and used it for a down payment for a house. Lisa had worked hard fixing her credit after I destroyed it for her. We were doing our finances separately because at least one of us would have credit. So we looked at houses for a few months and made some offers, and finally an offer was accepted. So this was good. We could finally move from the rental property into our own home. Lisa bought the house. John and I checked it out; it was a solid home but needed work. But we were used to that. Lisa's sisters came over and helped paint all the rooms. My job was the bathroom. I completely gutted it and remodeled it in ten days. Lisa was happy with it. It's still a nice bathroom. All the carpet came up, and I refinished the original hardwood floors. So we made the house livable and moved. This did help me for a while. It gave me a little self-worth. So after living there a while, I became even more comfortable with my warped, selfish lifestyle. The days kind of ran together. I would get up, go buy lotto tickets and beer, drive, look for scrap, and work if I had a job. My marital relationship was very strained. Lisa stopped harping at me because it made no difference. But Lisa was making her own plans. She wasn't going to continue living like this. I was spending hundreds of dollars a week on lotto tickets. I paid some bills, and I thought that made everything okay.

Well, I struck it kind of big and won nearly $10,000 in one week. So I decided I deserved a new truck, so I went to the dealer and put enough down to lease a new one. Now I looked good—F-150, four-wheel drive, V8, and nice wheels. I felt like I was okay again. It looked good to sell jobs. It was the perfect front. I used this nice new truck for hauling scrap, but I kept it looking good. I also picked up a new contract rehabbing rental homes. So I was working a lot and making okay money. But nothing changed. Same life, different day. Drink until I fell asleep. But I had a nice truck.

During this time, Lisa was making her own plans which I wasn't aware of and probably wouldn't have cared. She was looking at apartments and planning to move; something I didn't even know until years later. I didn't realize just how much anguish and frustration I was putting her through. She sacrificed a lot and put up with a lot for many years. Everyone has a limit as to how much they can take, and Lisa was at that limit. I now was fifty-five. Not violent or real mean, I just didn't care anymore. I had accepted that I would probably die from drugs and alcohol use, and I was okay with that. I wasn't suicidal, but killing myself slowly was okay. About two years before, my brother Ben died after spending four years in a nursing home. Ben was only two years older than me. We were very close. I always followed after Ben, and he taught me much. Ben also used a lot of drugs and alcohol. We started partying together at a very young age. We never got a clear diagnosis of what happened to Ben's health, but

I knew Ben as good as anyone. I knew what he used and what his bad habits were. I followed after Ben for many years, and we did a lot of things together. So I knew it was drugs and alcohol that took him away permanently. Ben was just fifty-five when he died—young by today's standards.

Here I was, fifty-five. I missed my brother and was very near to leaving as he had. You would think knowing this would straighten me out, but it didn't seem to make any difference. I was killing myself too. Deep down inside, I knew God could change everything, but I just wasn't willing to change my ways. But also by myself, I didn't have the ability to change my ways. I just wanted to live my way even if it killed me. How selfish I was. What about my wife? What about my kids? What about my grandkids? What about my other brothers and sisters and, last but not least, my parents who were gone now, had already seen me live my wild years, and would now see me like this? I just didn't see any of this because I had a full-time, around-the-clock job thinking about myself and how I felt. Such a sad, empty existence. My only hope was money. I really believed a lot of money would make me whole again. I still made a good appearance in public and put on a good front, but I was slowly slipping away. Lisa—bless her heart—decided there was one more thing that she could try. It was something that would take a lot of prayer, confidence, help, coordination, and cooperation; but she still loved me and wanted to save me from myself.

This plan would include my sister Sunny and my three kids. I don't know who all or what all were involved, but other family members and many people were praying. I knew nothing about the organizing going on.

The plan was an intervention complete with hope, detoxification, rehab, and recovery. Interventions do not always work. Sometimes they can backfire. Lisa and the family were aware of the risks. But what was the alternative? So far, nothing in my past had made any lasting difference. It was possible that it would save my life. The way I was going at this point, anything could happen, and I didn't seem to be worried about it. I had no idea that any of this was about to be initiated. I lived in a fog a lot of the time. I was enslaved and didn't care if I lived or died.

So Lisa approached me in a nonthreatening manner and asked me if I would be home on a particular night at a particular time. I asked what for, but she wouldn't tell me. She just said that it would be good, so I said okay, no problem. So I stayed sober for the meeting, being that I didn't know what it was. Then they all showed up—Sunny, Colette, Sam, Michael, and, of course, Lisa. I was happy to see everyone but a little apprehensive. Now I don't remember everything that was said that evening, but I remember how it made me feel. But they all had written a letter, which each of them read out loud. They spoke of the things that my addiction had caused, what it had done to me, how it affected them, and how much they love me and don't want to lose me. I could have easily taken this all sideways. But this was my family, and they sincerely cared about me and wanted the best for me and had made steps and sacrifices to help me. God was in the room because it melted my hard heart. Even though my mind was in a fog, it made a great impact to my heart. My oldest son, Sam, who had just been married a couple of years, stated that he was planning on having children and he wanted his children to know their grandfather and spend time with him. And Colette, who had two children, wanted them to know and learn from their grandfather. This made a huge impact deep in my soul. I was thinking, *What parent would let their child spend time with a drunken grandfather?* At this, I felt hurt, guilty, selfish, worthless, helpless, and lower than a snake's belly. They were all very sincere in the way they presented themselves. So many things were flashing through my mind. I'm a person who never cries. I have a cold, hard heart, but this brought tears to my eyes and my voice. I couldn't even respond. I just sat there in a trance listening and taking it all in. God was working on my heart, and the love of Jesus filled the room. The meeting only lasted about an hour but long enough to get the message across.

But they didn't dwell on that then. They moved on and told me about hope and a solution. Then they told me the plan. They had made arrangements with a rehab center in Atlanta, Georgia, and asked me if I would be interested. I said yes, I would but that I would need to go into detoxification. Sunny is a retired nurse and very knowledgeable in everything medically and said yes, that would be arranged. Lisa asked would I be willing, so I humbly accepted, realizing that this was my chance and the other choice didn't look too good. I said it would take a few weeks to finish my jobs and get prepared. Then Lisa made the expectations of me clear. I was expected to stop tomorrow and give up construction and all of what I was doing. This was a life change, and I needed to drop everything and put myself and recovery first. This was difficult for me. I was in the middle of a job and had taken money from the customer, and I had other loose ends to take care of. I had a new truck to pay for. I had debts, and my taxes were behind a few years and not filed. My garage was a mess, and the truck full of stuff. I had a long list of reasons for delays. But Lisa made it clear in a kind, firm, but resolute manner. She said nothing was more important at this time and that everything would be taken care of. At this, I reluctantly agreed and said I'd do whatever she asked of me.

Then I said, "I'm ready. I will do what I need to do because it's time to make a change. I've made a mess of things, and this must be the cause of my problems."

CHAPTER 8

Intervention

S O I STILL HAD a few days before the arrangements got started. So I worked around the house, garage, and my truck. I did the best I could at cleaning and organizing. I canceled and finished up the best I could with jobs I was working on. One job I had to return money and give the customer the news of why I couldn't do the work. It was about a week before detox could take me in. Lisa made an appointment with my doctor so he would be completely informed of our plan and also to be checked out. So this meant no more pain pills from doctor also. I found some pain pills of Lisa's from something that she had forgotten about. So I helped myself with them until detox. I was not able to stop on my own without help, so I kept doing what I had been. I was very uneasy about what was coming. None of it sounded fun or exciting. None of this was my idea of a vacation or adventure. My life was a mess; how did I get here? I was loaded with debt, back taxes, and a couple of years I didn't file. I didn't know if this was caused by just my addictions or I was just stupid. A lot was going through my mind. I was sad, depressed, guilty, anxious, and very apprehensive. But I felt I really didn't have much choice. I could just run, but I believed it was time to face truth and reality. I had let many people down, especially my wife. Even if I couldn't fix everything, it was time to make a change, and I was as ready as I had the ability to be.

The last night at home before going to Arrowhead, I got completely inebriated. I could hardly talk without slurring my words. Lisa was kind to me that night. She didn't get mad; she was just worried about me.

So the next morning, Lisa drove me out to Arrowhead. I still was in no condition to drive. Even knowing it was all gonna end, I had no power of my own to stop. These addictions had been, and still were, controlling me; and there was nothing I could do. I was defenseless against their power. When we arrived at Arrowhead, I met with a counselor, and she asked me a lot of questions, most of which I don't remember. But when that part was done, she said I was accepted for treatment. Then they took me to an examination room and told me to strip and put on a gown.

I objected and said, "Why do you expect this from me?"

The whole idea to me was humiliating and unnecessary, and on top of it, it was two ladies.

Then she said, "You might be hiding drugs on your body."

I responded, saying, "I'm here to get off drugs voluntarily. Why would I bring them with me?"

But she replied, saying patients had done it in the past and they needed to be sure. Very reluctantly, I gave in and let them search me. I sure was glad when that was over. Then they escorted me to the front desk of admittance for introductions and more questions.

When the nurse checked me, she said, "You're detoxing right now because your pupils are dilated."

So they treated me with a drug under my tongue for withdrawals; they proceeded showing me my accomidations for the week. They took me to the room where I would be sleeping. The room was very plain and uninviting; the bed was only about two feet wide with no sheets or blankets. It was not like a hospital or motel room. I didn't want to be there. A green vinyl mattress so narrow it seemed as though I'd roll right off. I was so discouraged by where I was, but no withdrawals. But I got down on my knees, put my elbows on that green mattress, and prayed.

I asked God, *How did I get here? Where did I go wrong? Please take these addictions from me, change me, teach me how to follow your will and not mine because my will got me here. In Jesus' name. Amen.*

They came and retrieved me from my room and showed me around. There was a TV room, but the channels were controlled by who was first. So the TV room was of no use to me. Then we all were escorted to the cafeteria for lunch. I was pleasantly surprised; the food was excellent—fruits, vegetables, and nutritious drinks and snacks. And you could eat all you wanted. I gotta say eating was the one thing I really looked forward to, and good food really helped healing. They were right on track. Our days were very busy, meeting all day with small breaks in between, but meetings were the main part of the day. At night, there was time to mingle or read or watch TV. But everything was regimented. In the meetings, there was a counselor. We filled out questionnaires and had discussions. Some days, we even had yoga, which was relaxing; but I got a little bored. I actually enjoyed the meetings and took everything I could from them. All the counselors were good, and the employees took their job seriously and compassionately.

I had good conversations with other patients. It helped pass the time in the evening. One patient told me he had been there seventeen times. It seemed Arrowhead had revolving doors for some patients. By the third day, I wanted to graduate out of there so I wouldn't take any more medication for withdrawal. God was helping me through this. Several times a day, I would be on my knees asking him to help me through this, and he did. So I let them know I was ready to leave. I would have to meet with a doctor and answer all their questions and show them I was ready. I was through withdrawals, but I still felt like crap and felt like something was missing and it was something I didn't need anymore. Detox was definitely a necessary step for me to get through this. It wasn't a horrible experience, but I knew I never wanted to do it again. I couldn't understand how a person could go through this seventeen times. Finally they were ready to release me five days, and the rewards for me going through this were exponential. But I was not going back. April 1, 2016, I walked out with Lisa on my side. I was quiet, humble, uncomfortable, but glad to head out into the sunlight. As I left the doors behind, God and I knew that my life had changed. I didn't know anything about what was in the future, but I knew I had changed and life would be different. It was something that I would keep to myself for a long time because nobody would take me seriously, but I knew that would carry me.

I thank God for the clarity that he gave me that day and a little peace of mind. April 1, 2016, is my sobriety anniversary date until today. I was not smiling and happy on this day because of the uncertainty of what was to come and the way I felt physically and mentally. So I stayed home for just a couple of days before my journey. Lisa kept close tabs on me, and I appreciated that because I didn't trust myself either. God was with me, that I knew, so I leaned on him. What time I had at home, I was praying and reading the Bible. This is where truth and answers come from, so I was searching with all my heart.

So arrangements were made by Sam, and Colette drove me to Detroit airport. A lot of work was going to be on Lisa's shoulders, and that made me feel even worse. But Lisa was prepared to do whatever she needed for my recovery. No words could express how I felt, but I was also scared. None of this was going to be fun for anybody, yet it was necessary. I didn't think life could ever be good again. I was a complete loser, addict, broke, in debt, and basically helpless. I was dependent on my family for all my basic needs. But at this point, the obsession for drugs and alcohol had been removed, but I felt an emptiness in my gut. But having the obsession removed was a miracle, and God was giving me some hope.

So I got on a plane and headed for Atlanta, Georgia. I wasn't supposed to have any money with me, but I took $21. When I arrived in Atlanta, it was arranged for me to be picked up at the airport. This whole experience was humiliating. I was a fish out of water. How did I end up here? Finally, a young man in a van found me and picked me up. The drive was about an hour. We talked, but he wouldn't tell me much. He was only there to retrieve me. When I arrived at NLB, I waited outside the office for nearly an hour. No one was there.

Finally someone showed up and let me in an office where I waited again. Finally he came back and asked me if I was hungry, which I was, so he brought me a plate of food. I didn't know what it was. It was awful; I could barely eat half of it. Finally three guys showed up and introduced themselves. They brought me into a conference room and asked me a lot of questions. I was not accepted yet until I passed the interview. I couldn't understand what they wanted. I was an alcoholic and addict and wanted to be fixed. What else was there to know?

Finally, they pushed the right buttons and brought me to tears, then I caught myself and apologized.

One of the guys said to me, "Never apologize for crying."

That was what they were looking for. They wanted to know if I had a conscience or remorse. Either way, that's when they said they would accept me into their program. From there, they showed me to my accommodations, a bedroom with many beds which you needed to earn your way to the more comfortable one. So my bed was an upper in the corner with a lower ceiling. Now I am claustrophobic, and it was scary and difficult to get in and out of. Then they showed me the bathrooms—beat up, falling apart, but reasonably clean because everyone has bathroom detail. We all met up in the cafeteria where I met other addicts and alcoholics. I was definitely one of the older ones there, not the oldest but close. Fifty-five is pretty old to be at a place like this. Some of the guys were okay. A lot of them acted like they were better than me. That's because they had been there a while earning trust and privileges. So you could say I was quite uncomfortable and didn't feel like I fit in. I was part of a group which I met with in a small room and talked about all kinds of things.

The next day, I was taken to my new job. Everyone had to work forty hours a week. If you did something wrong, like leaving the bedroom light on the last one out, you would have to work Saturday. My job was working with used clothes for the thrift store. I disliked this job very much. I asked if I could do something different because I'm mechanical and good with tools. They told me I had no say in the matter and they decided where I would work.

The reason why the food was so awful was because all the food was donated by local grocery stores. Sometimes the food was okay, but a lot of it wasn't. It was cooked by other addicts that had been promoted. The coffee was the worst coffee I've ever had in my life, but it was something everyone there needed. It was like they put ten times the normal amount to get maximum caffeine. But there wasn't any creamer, just one-percent milk, so nothing could make it tolerable. So the atmosphere was punishment. I understood it to a degree, but they took it too far. In my short stay at NLB, there was one thing I took with me which I thought was great.

Each day, we were expected to journal and fill the space we were given, and we were given an hour. I journaled straight for eight months of recovery, and I still do. It had helped me for writing this book. There were positive results brought out through this program. There were many young men who had complete life changes. I just didn't think I deserved this punishment, and it wasn't going to work for me. We spent too much time working our forty-hour job plus we had chores to do.

CHAPTER 9

Wilderness

I THOUGHT WE SHOULD BE going to a lot of meetings daily, but we weren't. We attended one or two meetings at night after working. We were tired. I could have stayed home to be a work-aholic. I wanted to work on my recovery, not folding clothes and cleaning bathrooms and cafeterias. Finally, I made a decision that I wasn't staying and started packing my bag. Around there, nothing went unnoticed. Someone was always watching what you're doing. Several guys pulled me aside and talked to me, attempting to change my mind. But I just didn't want to be there. It could be up to a year, and that was too much for me. I knew this was probably a mistake, but there just was no turning back now.

So my last stop on my way out was to see the director being that he had my wallet and cell phone. Also what little money I had in it. So I was up early and on my way to the office with my book bag packed tight.

After arriving, one of the administrators said to me, "So you're gonna leave."

I said, "Yes. I would like to collect my personal belongings."

Then the director showed up to see me off. Word got around fast there. They were both expecting me.

Then the director told me, "If you leave, you won't be allowed back."

Maybe he was bluffing, maybe not. They would probably let me back if I begged.

I said, "Maybe if I'm out for a few days, I'll decide to come back."

But he assured me I would not be allowed back. Anyway, I knew I would never beg to come back, but I was contemplating.

Then the administrator said, "I can see you've made up your mind. What are you gonna do, eat raw fish?"

Wow, obviously he had no idea about my survival skills. I certainly know how to build a fire to cook my fish. All that statement did was to increase the challenge factor for me.

Then the administrator told me, "You're insane. You're just a bum."

This just told me what he and this place thought of me. Maybe it was true, but negative reinforcement has never worked on me. So he made up my mind for me.

"I'll take my things, and I'm going."

So the administrator handed me my wallet and phone and counted out $21. Then I walked out. I had been humiliated enough over the last month. Now it was time to do it my way. As I started walking, I had remorse. I knew they would contact Lisa and tell her I walked out. I didn't want to worry my family and disappoint them after all they had done for me. But I planned to recover. My life had changed, and now it would even be harder to prove myself. I had no concrete plan, but I would travel north and be back home eventually. My cell phone had been shut off, so there was no way to make a call for now.

As I left with no map or direction, I just went by instinct and tried to go north. I was carrying a lot, boots and shoes hanging off my book bag which couldn't carry any more. So this was day one of my journey home. A nice day, hot Georgia weather. I couldn't spend money wastefully. Walking mile after mile on unknown highways wasn't that fun. I was thirsty and hungry and still uncomfortable from many years of addictions. But no matter what, I wasn't going back, and I couldn't go home. I had burnt all my bridges. It was time to take care of myself.

I attempted to hitchhike, but everyone was in a hurry. So far, Atlanta people seemed not to be friendly to strangers. So I prayed a lot while walking, asking God for direction and wisdom. As I walked, I became really thirsty. I looked, and there was a bottled water standing on the curb. I picked it up and drank it, taking the bottle with me for refills. It didn't matter to me that someone else drank from it. This was about survival now, and I was thankful. I walked by a gas station, and they allowed me to refill my water bottle. It felt like I walked about thirty miles on day one, so I needed to find a place to rest for the night. It was getting toward dark. I was exhausted and drained by hunger when I came to a small bridge over a stream. As I looked up stream, I saw a small wooded area, a good place to stay for the night. I waited until there was no traffic. I didn't want anyone to spot me walking in. So I tucked back in under some trees. It was secluded enough. The only drawback was that it bordered a school about seventy-five yards away, but no one could see me. But I couldn't build a fire until after dark as to draw any attention. By now, Lisa and family were informed of my departure and were not very happy about it. My sister Sunny prayed that it would rain tonight, and maybe I would go back. So before it got dark, I collected firewood so as to start a fire after dark. As soon as it turned dark, Sunny's prayer was answered, and it started raining. I had no camping equipment, blankets, tarps, or anything but a bedsheet. So I tied the sheet to tree branches for rain fly and clothes for blankets and pillow. It rained all night, and the wind picked up. I got up several times in the night to search for wet, mushy firewood. But I kept the fire going until morning. It was smoky but gave me some warmth and light. At this point, maybe I should've turned around to go back to NLB. I could cry, apologize, and beg. Maybe they would allow me back in. But stubbornness and pride are strong characteristics or flaws of mine. No way was I turning back. I was up early the next morning because I barely slept. All my belongings were soaked. I had no food or water. I was very sore, uncomfortable, and humbled. So before doing anything, I read my Bible, got on my knees, and prayed, asking God for direction, wisdom, and his plan for me. Then I packed up early and trudged out of there, careful not to be noticed by passersby. So as I walked estimating North while I prayed continually throughout my day.

God, here I am. Don't know where I am going or what I'm doing, but I'm listening now.

About a half mile from where I camped, I came to a store with a dollar rack. I bought just a few dollars' worth of the most nourishing snacks I could get and refilled my water bottle. After that, I walked all day on two-lane country roads; the only direction was north. Day two of my journey was uneventful, hot, dry, and mile after mile of country land and farmland with no interaction with anyone. I did encounter one main highway for a couple of miles. As I came to an overpass and being tired from carrying my belongings, I decided it was time to shed some excess weight. I had been carrying my favorite cowboy boots which I had bought when I was seventeen. So I set them there neatly hoping someone in need would find them and put them back into use. I still miss those boots until today. As my day was coming to an end, it was difficult to find a good camping spot. No rivers or bridges. Mostly private-owned land. But I had to stop somewhere as it was approaching dark.

So finally I picked a spot—no houses to be seen and a hill to hide me from the road. Dry firewood was plentiful; it had never been used for camping. I was hidden from the road and slept on a slope. After dark, I built a hot, dry fire as to not draw attention and I ended up getting a good night's sleep. I did get up early, said my prayers, and moved on. Even though it seemed risky, it was a better night than my first night.

After about a couple of hours of walking, I came to the city of Cumming, Georgia. This is when things started to get interesting for me. Some good, some not so good. First I came to a Fast Fuel convenience stop, and I wanted a large coffee. It was already hot, and when I walked in past the ice-cold beer with glass doors sweating, it called out to me. I thought about it for a second. I'm sure they would've tasted good, but I got what I came in for. Outside tables and chairs were a good place to read, write, and enjoy the first good cup of coffee in weeks. While I was there, I was deciding my next step and decided to find a church willing to help me out. So I headed down Ronald Reagan Boulevard until I found a United Methodist Church. So I went to the office and rang the bell. Two nice ladies working there invited me in and offered me a cup of coffee. I graciously accepted the coffee and proceeded to tell them bits of my story and what I needed. The two ladies were very accommodating. They gave me a complimentary food-care package that was made up ahead of time. It included peanut butter, jelly, canned goods, vegetables, fruits, and drinks—enough to last several days if managed. Also, they helped me with directions, so I had some idea where I was and where I might be heading. So I thanked them, packed up, and headed out.

So from there, I walked about a mile and stopped to rest, now carrying more weight, which was difficult with my lack of equipment. As I was sitting there, three police cars stormed up with their lights on toward me as if I was a criminal. The officers came to me with serious expressions on their faces. They started grilling me, asking all kinds of questions, asking me if I was packing drugs or any white powder. I didn't understand what they were getting at about white powder. They wanted to know where I came from and where I stayed the previous night. I was being as evasive as I could with these questions, remembering I had built a fire on some farmers' land. This whole thing seemed ridiculous. Why were they harassing me? Then they asked to call my wife, and I reluctantly gave them her number. Lisa answered the call. She didn't know how to respond. She didn't know what I was up to or into. I hadn't talked to her. She only knew I was gone. After that, they searched my bags wearing rubber gloves. What the heck were they looking for? Finally they realized they were interrogating the wrong person. They told me someone threw white powder in the mailbox of the church I had just came from.

After the interrogation was completed, one of the officers drove me about five miles away to the edge of town. In a polite way, he was telling me to leave his town. So he dropped me off, said good luck, and was on his way. Now I was on the other end of town. I had no idea where I was, and it was late in the day.

So all I could do was walk in the direction away from town. It seemed my earlier day plans had changed, whatever they were. As I walked the rural business highway, I saw a small wooded area off the side, thinking it was a good place to rest in the shade. As I entered the woods, I spotted a bicycle lying on its side. So I sat for a while, thinking and contemplating about the bicycle. A bike would be very helpful, but I didn't want to end up in the Cumming jail. No money. No one to bail me out. As I examined the bike, I noticed weeds had grown through the spokes, and tires were almost flat. This bike had been here for a while, probably abandoned for whatever reason.

So I prayed about it, then came up with a plan. So I took the bike, took it to a tire store, aired up the tires, and searched for a camping spot. I found a small river down in a gully with a lot of foliage to hide me from the highway. So that night, I tied everything to the bicycle, ate good, cleaned up, and tried to get some sleep. So I awoke early, packed up, and moved on. God was looking out for me and provided me with a bicycle.

The objective was to get as far away from Cumming as quickly as possible, and that is what I did. The bicycle wasn't as comfortable as driving but it sure beat walking. That day, I wanted to look different so the Cumming police didn't recognize me if I crossed their path. So I shaved, cleaned up, didn't wear my hat, and chose clothing different from the previous day. I did not want to be noticed leaving, so I took all possible precautions. I pedaled hard and fast to leave that city. My destination was Gainesville, Georgia. It was only twenty-five to thirty miles, but it was very hot going into a strong wind. The bicycle was heavy with mountain tires. So after I was at a safe distance from Cumming, it was time to stop for some rest. I stopped in front of a hot dog restaurant just opening. It was set back in about a hundred feet. So I pulled out my water bottle and book which I had been reading. It was a strange-looking place. It looked like a doghouse; and it was called the Dog House with tables, chairs, and umbrellas out front. As I was reading, a good-looking Black man came walking out toward me. I was thinking he was probably going to yell at me and tell me to get away from his property, that I would scare his customers away. After Cumming, I still had a sour taste in my mouth, but that was not what happened at all.

The man walked up, handed me a five-dollar bill, then said, "I know sometimes people go through rough times in their life, and I understand."

So I thanked him.

Then he said, "How about a hot dog?"

I told him I couldn't afford a hot dog. I had some food and water in my pack.

Then he said, "No, this is on me. Come on up. Sit down under the umbrella. Relax and enjoy a hot dog on me."

It turned out that he and his wife owned this establishment, and they both worked there. They were both very friendly and accommodating. So I took a seat; and after a few minutes, I was served two hot dogs, fries, and an ice-cold Coca-Cola. When I finished, I cleaned up after myself, went back to the window, and thanked them again for their hospitality. Everything was so good—the best hot dogs I've ever had. I didn't realize how hungry and thirsty I really was. I wolfed every last bite down. God put those people in my path that day to encourage me and to help me see the good in his people.

When I left, I was encouraged, and my energy restored. After that, I pedaled all the way to Gainesville. I had a headwind. The heat was intense, but I was invigorated. I entered the outskirts of Gainesville in midafternoon. My plan was to find a church open and get times and directions for an AA meeting. Of course, I knew no one and didn't know where I would stay, but going to a meeting was my top priority today. AA was going to be a big part of my recovery, and I was serious about that. So I found a church open, and they were very helpful. I obtained the information I needed. The meeting was at 8:00 p.m., about seven more miles. While on my way to meeting, I saw a Verizon store, so I stopped in to activate my cellphone. That was a tough seven miles of uphill, but I still arrived nearly two hours early.

So I rested under a shade tree, did some reading, looked my bicycle over and then I noticed a bulge in my tire; so I knew my miles were limited in this condition. So I needed to think about some things after the meeting, but the meeting was first. So as soon as the doors opened, I entered, got some coffee, and introduced myself. People were friendly, sincere, and interested. Like most AA meetings, I really enjoyed myself and felt at home. These were people a lot like me who understood what I was going through. I didn't share my story with the group. I just stayed quiet and listened during the meeting. But the meeting was so calming to my spirit, hearing others sincerely share their strengths, experience, and hope. When it was over, I just wanted to come back again. It was just the right medicine that I really needed at this time. After the meeting, I stood around outside shaking hands and talking with other alcoholics, knowing I didn't know what I was going to do tonight as it now was dark. As everyone else was clearing out, there was one older man—gray hair and long gray beard—standing around, and he started talking with me. He was wise, intelligent, and interested in my circumstances. As we were talking, I pulled my bicycle out of its hiding spot, and he was quite interested in my story. As we were talking, I showed him my tire and talked a little about my journey. His name was Duane.

He said, "Put your bike in my truck. Let's go to Walmart and get a tire."

So while Duane drove me to Walmart, we had a good conversation, I told him what had happened with NLB at Walmart, he bought me a new tire and tube. After we left there, he asked me where I was going tonight, which I responded, "I don't know." Then Duane offered me to sleep in his garage for the night, which I answered, "Sure, that would be great. Thank you." He said it was nothing fancy, but it was safe and out of the weather, and I agreed.

I ended up living in Duane's garage for about three weeks. Duane and I went to two meetings nearly every day at the same place. These meetings helped to put some consistency back into my life. Duane was also a minister and very devout in his beliefs. Sometimes I would go to his church with him. But I found a church I really liked and would go on Wednesday night—the Free Chapel, a large church with modern music and a great pastor speaking from the Bible. Duane didn't like me going to other churches. We also did some small jobs so that I could earn a little money. I also used my cell phone and called Lisa a couple of times. Lisa had a hard time understanding what I was doing, and I had no clear-cut answer. I told her I was going to a lot of meetings and church and that I was still sober. But I also said I didn't know when or if I would come back to Toledo. I didn't know what my future would be, but I knew I couldn't go home. Duane and I got along really good at first, but after a while, he would get really angry toward me. Even though we both believed in the Bible, we both interpreted it differently.

Duane was a minister and spoke well to the congregation. So at first, I just agreed with everything he would say. But after a while, our differences were too big for me to stay silent anymore. He believed that all churches other than his would go to hell. Also, if you weren't baptized, you would go to hell. He also believed that miracles couldn't happen anymore. All three of these beliefs I just couldn't agree to and was quite vocal about it, but I didn't get angry. Also, he was my sponsor. One day, he got so angry at me I thought he was going to hit me.

My response was "Your anger is out of control. If I can't discuss my thoughts with you, you can't be my sponsor." Then I said, "Besides, we are friends, and this isn't how you treat your friend."

He responded, "I'm not your friend. I'm your sponsor. And if I'm not your sponsor, then I can't trust you, so it's time for you to move on."

So I agreed to leave in the morning. The funny thing is I was always 100 percent honest with Duane. I did a lot of work on his house which he said he would pay me for and never did. But he had no reason to not trust me. He was just angry at me because I wouldn't agree to his philosophy. Growing up, we went to church three times a week, studied the Bible, and memorized scripture; and I had read the Bible through at least two times as an adult. Just because someone gets angry at me and attempts to bully me into his way of thinking and believing about deep rooted issues, and I am already stubborn in nature. Besides, the only way I will change my biblical belief structure is when it is pointed out to me in scripture, and even then, I will research it myself.

This does not mean I think I know everything about the Bible because I don't, but I stand firm on what I know. But anyway, it was time to move on. It wasn't all bad. A lot of good came from my three weeks in Gainesville. I did still manage to hang on to $200, and my bicycle was ready to go. Duane told me to have breakfast with him in the morning before I leave, but that wasn't my plan. That night, I packed up the bicycle, so I'd be ready as soon as I awake. I left before 6:00 a.m., pedaled about three miles to a Waffle House, and paid for a large breakfast to give me energy for the day.

So after a good breakfast, I stopped at a park on a lake to clean up, rest, and spend a little time with prayer and reading, also killing a little time before going to a noon AA meeting before getting out of Gainesville. I knew Duane didn't usually go to the noon meeting. I really didn't want to see him. But I had gotten to know some of the people there, and I always enjoyed the meetings. So after the meeting, I left Gainesville, heading north again. There was good weather ahead; and I was not in a hurry plus, at least, I had a couple hundred bucks to travel on. I was still thinking about how things had worked out with Duane. He was a good guy but had some serious anger and bitterness issues. When I first met him, I thought he was very wise—wiser than me—after all I have done, the numerous failures in my past. He attempted to pound his ideals and beliefs into me and was angered at my response. Then he would remind me of my failures.

But this didn't work on me, minister or not. I think I had a clearer understanding of God's Word than he did. The only way I will change my mind on the Scripture is if they show me a scripture, but he didn't. I think this was God's way of showing me that I was on the right track. But I also know that praying and studying God's Word daily is of utmost importance toward fully productive spiritual life.

But still another bridge burnt. What was I doing? Where was I going? That was the main reason for stopping at the park and going to one more meeting. I felt lost and rejected, and I needed direction. So in the park, I read the Bible, prayed, and meditated, just asking God what was next. Whatever was next, I would wait for the answer and just keep going, waiting for inspiration.

So I wasn't too concerned about covering too many miles, but I wanted a good place to camp. I pedaled about thirty miles to a city called Dahlonega. *Dahlonega* is a Cherokee Indian word meaning "yellow" or "gold." Dahlonega and all of Lumpkin County was the site of the first major gold rush in our nation. This town was hilly, well kept, and a historical district and had good restaurants and places to stay. If I wasn't homeless, this would be a great place to visit, stay, and learn more of their heritage. But I was homeless, with no money to waste, looking for a free place to stay. Wouldn't you know, another flat tire. So I was pushing my bike uphill, not sure what to do. Just then, a car pulled over and stopped.

A good-looking young man, about twenty, jumped out and said, "Hey, you need some help?"

"Yeah, I sure could."

We introduced ourselves to each other. The young man's name was Joe, in the National Guard, off for a couple of days.

He said, "Put your bike in the trunk. I'll take you to Walmart and get you a tire."

"Okay, thanks. I really appreciate it."

While riding, he told me he just got engaged. He seemed a top-notch lad. We went into Walmart. He bought me a tire, tube, and Vise-Grips and helped me repair my bicycle. Then he took me to a public park and showed me where to camp that no one would bother me. So he left after shaking hands and saying goodbye and good luck. It wasn't an easy spot to get to, long downhill trail needing to carry the bicycle down. But once there on a little river, it was crystal clear. I set up what I had, built a nice fire, and stocked up for the night. Didn't have much to eat, only water and couple of snacks. By now, I was tired. It ended up a long day and dark by the time I was settled. But rethinking the day, God kept bringing good people into my life; and for that, I was thankful. Every day I was being cared for, from morning to night. Things just worked out. When I woke up in the morning, noticing poison ivy all around me, even above me in the trees, I figured it was time to get moving out. I packed up and carried my bicycle up the steep, grueling incline with tree roots and logs for footing. By the time I made it up, I was sweating and out of breath.

I thought next time I'd look for an easier spot. But this was just the beginning of the hardest day of all my travels. Joe had told me that the direction I was heading was all uphill. He was being truthful. Dahlonega is the starting point of the Appalachian Trail heading up into the mountains. When I left, I thought there would be places to stop for food and water, so I didn't have much. As soon as I was out of town, I was going uphill, and that never changed. I tried pedaling, but it was just too steep. So I was pushing. To make things less easy, it was very hot with no breeze. As difficult as the trail was, I believe this day was detoxifying for me. I was sweating all day with no food, only water, then I ran out of water. No place to rest, straight up on my right, and straight down on my left. If I had to camp, I couldn't. I could only keep going. About the time I was getting dehydrated and exhausted, I came to a small waterfall. There was a small parking area with a sign that said "Don't drink the water." Well, of course, I ignored the sign. I stood under the fall and cooled down. What an answer to prayer. I rested there a bit, drank what I could, and filled my water bottle. I couldn't say that I felt good so soon into my recovery, but this was good for my body after all the years of abuse. After feeling a little invigorated, I headed back to pushing again. It didn't change—never down, only up. It seemed it would never end. Then came dark clouds. It was about to storm, and I had no defense. Then the wind picked up and rain started to pour. Then a bridge appeared out of nowhere. Not really, I was sure it was probably always there, but the timing couldn't have been more perfect because it was God's timing. So I took shelter under the bridge overlooking a small river. It looked late in the day, so I figured I would spend the night there. This really wasn't the perfect spot to stay. Ground was rocky and bumpy and not very private. People driving by could see me.

Then the rain stopped. The sun came out, and it was beautiful again. So I decided to take a chance and keep traveling, maybe find a better spot. So on and on, I was pushing uphill again, thinking maybe I should have stayed under the bridge. It was like earlier—no place to stop. Now I was pushing in the dark, starting to get a little concerned. My legs were so sore that they were going numb; my back was killing me (figuratively speaking), and I had no food or water.

This is when I really realized that mountain miles are much different than straight, flat highway miles. I don't think that I had traveled near as far as it felt like I had. Many fears were flashing through my mind as headlights were beaming up behind me. Unexpectedly, a blue minivan pulled up next to me stopped, and the passenger side window opened up. A concerned gentle voice called out, "You look tired," then I responded, "Yes, I am. It has been a long day." Then I asked, "Do you know how far to the next town?" Then she answered, saying, "It's quite a distance yet. Why don't you load your bicycle and I'll give you a lift."

"Yeah, that sounds great."

In all my years of hitchhiking and traveling, I've never had a woman pick me up. This was very unusual, but there's more. I don't remember her name. We had a nice conversation, but she didn't try to pry into my story like many do. She just told me she was going to Blue Ridge to pick her daughter up first, then she could drop me off at Walmart. We drove for more than thirty minutes, picked up her daughter, then went to Walmart. We arrived at Walmart. She handed her daughter a credit card and told her take me in and get me whatever I needed. These people were not rich; her minivan had rust holes and high mileage. But this woman was compelled to do this act of kindness. The daughter took me into the store and bought me ham, cheese, bread, chips, cookies, and drinks. I thanked them both, and they were on their way. Every day, God was bringing people like this into my life. I said goodbye and thanked them sincerely.

By the time we were done in Walmart, it was raining. Talking to a Walmart employee, I was told there would be storms for two days and heavy rain.

So now I had a problem again. It was time to use some of the money I earned in Gainesville. Returning into the store, I bought a sleeping bag, a large tarp, bag of bungees, two packs of flashlights with batteries included, and a poncho. Altogether I spent under $50. A Walmart employee gave me a case of water. I had so much stuff I didn't know how to carry it especially in this weather, and where would I go? Well, I couldn't stay in Walmart, so I ventured out. I could barely even see but headed out of the parking lot. When I approached the main drive, there was a field across the street, commercial real estate for sale. The field was weeded and full of small evergreen trees, Christmas-tree size. It looked big enough to be able to hide, but definitely no fires. So I walked back in out of sight. First thing, a tarp. I folded it like a business letter, attached bungees to trees, and closed off the ends. Bicycle stayed out; everything else in. It was like a cocoon closed up. It was dry, and a sleeping bag made it comfortable with weeds underneath. I stayed two nights, plenty to eat. The next day, I went back to Walmart and bought a cheap AM/FM radio and enjoyed coffee from a nearby gas station. It sure was nice to have just the minimal camping gear. Although I was a little comfortable, I was still detoxing from the many years of drugs and alcohol. There was an emptiness in my head and stomach that no amount of comfort would cure. Only time could cure this with the help of God to get me through and keep me strong. But I didn't know this yet. I only knew how I felt. Here I was in this beautiful country and had a difficult time thoroughly enjoying the full magnitude of its splendor. So all I could do was to keep moving, praying, reading, and searching for answers. But good things were happening to me. For many miles, I pushed uphill following the Appalachian Trail. I pushed myself past my physical limits and then some. I tapped into raw determination that I didn't know I was capable of. I didn't know what all this meant yet, but I just kept going. I did know that God was meeting my needs daily. Though every day was uncomfortable and unpredictable, I do believe it was just the right medicine for a selfish, stubborn character as I. Yet it wasn't my plan. I never would've imagined this as my future. In my younger years, I never would believe that drugs and alcohol could rob me and my family of so much. Now I'm blessed with much time to think, pray, and reflect. What a gift.

I really needed those couple of days' rest by the Walmart. I estimated a total of about sixty to eighty miles from Gainesville. But I needed to move on. But the forecast for rain wasn't good, so I needed to be prepared for another night of rain. I found a nice spot on a lake but I didn't feel safe because there was a public road only about fifty feet away so I decided not to build a fire. So I covered up with the tarp and went to sleep early while it rained all night. You know, traveling into these strange towns and cities which I had never visited previously, it made me hesitant, wary, and a little nervous. I was always expecting to be visited by strangers unwanted and property owners or the local sheriff to harass me. After all, I was an uninvited stranger myself. Why would anyone trust me or want me there? Every time I chose a new camping spot, many thoughts would go through my mind. But it was the only way I was able to travel. I felt like a bum or hobo or whatever you would choose to call me. So when I came into contact with nice people, it really meant a lot to me. Last night's spot was no exception. I was too nervous to build a fire, and I laid my tarp flat to be less visible.

So after leaving the little lakefront spot, I continued north arriving near the Tennessee border. Today was another long, hot, and uphill day. A nice guy named Tim pulled off the road and offered me water and snacks, which I graciously accepted. So I made it to McCaysville, just south of the Tennessee border. The heat and hard work caused me to use up most of my food and water. So I reluctantly found another spot for the night on a small river. It appeared to have been used before by, possibly, local fishermen. There were small houses on the other side, so again I did my best to be as inconspicuous as possible. I built a small fire for light and to warm up canned goods, just waiting for the local sheriff to roll up and deciding how I'd explain myself.

So in the morning, I didn't stick around. I packed up and got out of there. By now, I was out of food and water. It looked pretty desolate heading into the Cherokee National Forest. I was able to get some free maps from a welcome center back in Blue Ridge, so I was using them now. I needed to know what I was heading into.

The next stretch I would be traveling would be over one hundred miles; ninety-three miles following the Ocoee River, well known for its white-water rafting. Very few stops in between except many roadside parks along the way. A very scenic ride. Several dams along the way but still a fast-running river. The good part of this ride was that it was a gradual descent following the river downstream.

After reviewing the maps, I knew I needed to have provisions. Nowhere to find them until Cleveland, two days away. If I had a better bicycle with less weight and better equipment, it could be done in a long day, but I figured two. It was time to find another church. I found a large Baptist church in McCaysville. So I stopped and rang the bell. They let me in, and the pastor came in to talk with me. They asked me to fill out a questionnaire; the pastor was interested in my story. He recommended I go home to my family. He then prayed for me and gave me a box of groceries. It was very basic food which needed a kitchen, but I took what I could use and thanked them. It was enough to sustain and nourish me for a couple of days, and that was enough.

So I left, crossed the border, and went into Tennessee. After about five miles, I came to Ducktown with a gas station carryout. Went to the dumpster and found a piece of cardboard to make a sign. I wrote these words on the sign: "Skilled Laborer. Need Work. Phone Number." I attached this sign to my back. I was getting low on cash. It was time to make some money. I also filled my water bottles before I left there. Here I was traveling through some of the most beautiful country I had ever seen and received very little enjoyment from it. All my past failures and mistakes kept flooding through my mind. I was lost and homeless, traveling around begging for food. I'm over fifty-five years old. What a loser I had become. Too old to start over so I thought I felt so alone. This should be fun, but it wasn't. Maybe if I could find a place to stay and get some work, maybe that would be a little better. So I thought, with a sign on my back, at least I was trying. So I traveled on, hoping something good would happen. Late in the afternoon, I started looking for places to stop. I hadn't eaten all day. I needed a fire to warm something up. I stopped several times to scope out the territory but wasn't satisfied with the privacy, lack of firewood, and difficulty of access. I finally found a spot—difficult access but met all other criteria. Almost dark by the time I got back in there. Right on the river, there was more firewood than I could use. Not visible from the highway, this would work for the night.

To the reader, I would really like to offer some insight into my purpose of writing this book.

First of all, it is an accounting of many blunders throughout my life and the recovery, rebuilding and the changing of my life. We all have a choice on how we choose to live. The question is, What do we choose? A person's decisions can change his destiny. My hope is that your reading is interesting, intriguing, informative, enlightening, hopeful, and inspiring. Also I hope to shed light on how powerful the progression of drugs and alcohol, how drugs and alcohol change your thinking, and the problems it can cause with money, security, relationships, psychologically, mentally, and physically. But then mending relationships and bringing security and stability back to the household. How to live a life of satisfaction, happiness, and fulfillment; to live longer and healthier; and to live for a purpose bigger than yourself.

In the beginning, drugs and alcohol were big fun for me. They were new; it was an adventure. But it doesn't take long before the destruction starts. The fun and happiness is just superficial; the friends that come along with it are too. When the happiness and friends erode away, what you have left are addictions and destruction. The addictions can be very difficult to shake on your own, and much of the destruction is unrepairable. When I was young, I didn't believe that could happen to me, but it did. It progressed, dragging me down slowly, no matter how hard I fought it; but I eventually found rock bottom.

My main purpose of this book is hope. There is a better way. With true happiness, you can live longer and healthier and have stronger relationships, caring for others more than yourself. It doesn't all happen overnight—living sober, following God's will, and making rational decisions and choices. It's all possible if that's what you are seeking.

So I camped on Ocoee River, had a nice hot fire all night, and caught up on eating with canned goods. You know, I never even thought about bears, but I was fortunate I wasn't visited at night. I was being protected even when I was careless. When I awoke, I had a filling breakfast before another long day. Then I spent time reading the Bible, praying, and meditating. I asked for direction, wisdom, and a way to earn some income.

So after getting packed up, devotions, and breakfast, I headed out with the sign on my back. After traveling just a little distance, a black Dodge Ram pickup with a diesel fuel tank and nozzle in the back pulled over in front of me a ways. A man stepped out and stood there, waiting for me to catch up. So I stopped. We each introduced ourselves and shook hands.

Eric said, "I saw your sign for work, and I need someone right now."

He asked me if I knew anything about chickens, to which I responded, "No, I don't."

He said it was hard work but plenty of it, if I didn't mind that.

"Well, I have no experience in that kind of work, but I'll work hard and learn."

I told him I was very mechanical and could fix things.

So we both agreed, and he gave me directions. He was on his way to work. So I was to meet his father named Dudley at the farm. He lived next door and also gave me his phone number if I needed help with directions. So he moved on, and I moved on happy and motivated. Maybe my sign had paid off. Man, it wasn't easy finding the farm—more than ten miles away from town out in farm country. But I finally made it late afternoon and met Dudley, and he put me straight to work. Apparently, they had a worker that up and quit, but his work was mediocre anyway. He always had excuses not to work.

He was telling me the truth: working with chickens is hard work. Three large buildings—300 feet by 100 feet, about three football fields—and over 300,000 chickens. About as far as you can see, all chickens. Each building had computer monitoring, but the computers didn't do any work. They only told you some of the problems. There were many mechanical aspects to the job, and one person could never keep up with the many, many chores and repairs. Moisture from chickens caused corrosion to steel cables, pulleys, and everything made of steel. Each building had twelve large fans with automatic venting to keep a negative air pressure, essential to keep chickens alive; rows and rows of drinkers and feeders to the full length of the buildings; and also two rows of gas heaters, full length of the building. Also air-conditioning air starts at ninety degrees when they are young to seventy degrees by the time they're mature. It only takes twelve to fourteen weeks to take them to market.

Drinkers, feeders, and heaters were suspended by cables and needed to be adjusted daily as chickens grow. After chickens were harvested, everything was cranked to the ceiling so barns could be cleaned and sprayed and bedding replaced. Often these steel cables and pulleys would break while being adjusted. As the only employee there, I had a full-time job.

Later that first night, Eric showed up at the farm when he was done working. After we discussed my duties, expectations, and pay, he asked me where I'd been staying. I asked if I could stay in chicken house computer room or camp out.

Then he said, "Come with me. I have a place for you."

We drove to his home, a mobile home about a quarter mile down the road. He told me I could use the couch, showed me the bathroom and kitchen, told me to make myself at home, and gave me a key. I didn't expect this kind of treatment. Eric was very trusting, more than I would ever be. Eric lived by himself, had been divorced, and wasn't in a hurry to remarry again. So at this point, my situation wasn't too bad. He would leave before 6:00 a.m., so he would be gone before I woke up.

I was happy to have the work and a place to stay with a shower and kitchen. I gave Eric no reason to mistrust me after his trust. I took my new job seriously and gave it 100 percent. Besides what I did inside, there was outside work also. He had a backhoe and several tractors. There was always more than enough work to do.

So during the next few months down on the farm, I put myself into my work, putting in up to seventy hours a week. I would go back and forth to the home, working after midnight and there by 7:00 a.m. They also added another chore—taking care of hogs and a mule, a daily job. I used a Yamaha utility truck to get back and forth. During this time, I never consumed any alcohol or drug. I stayed on course with recovery. But there were no AA meetings to go to, or I had no way to get there. I never discussed my past with Eric and Dudley, and they didn't pry. They were both happy with my progress, and the chickens were coming along very well. Now chickens died every day, and I was responsible for removing carcasses and documenting. Sometimes the numbers were high, so I worked hard to keep those numbers down. But no matter what I did, every day I disposed of them. The chickens were owned by a big chicken distributor; our job was to raise them. So they had inspectors stopping by periodically. They also did immunization for them through the feed and water system. So the company would pay by the pound for healthy chickens. The inspector told me and Eric that I was the best person he'd ever had taking care of the chickens. So I had a very busy job and was responsible for much, but I embraced the challenge. I was also fixing things like their backhoe and other things around there they had been putting off for a long time.

So for now, I had a good thing going. Dudley and I got along good. I met at his house every morning for coffee. Also he would tote me around for groceries, laundry, and whatever. But I was restless. This was not where my life was, but for now, I saved as much money as I could. I would call Lisa about once a week or so, but our conversations weren't always good. She didn't understand what I was doing, and I didn't either. But I told her I couldn't come back to Toledo and I didn't even know if I would. I assured her though that I was clean and sober and planned to stay that way. I needed to work because I had nothing, and I needed to build something. But who would believe me with my past history? So this was where I would stay for now until I figured out what I would do next.

After about a month, I started looking for cars. I was used to having my own transportation. Out in the country, there weren't a lot of options. One day, when Dudley and I were going to town, I spotted a little Chevy S-10 pickup truck for sale by owner for 850 with a phone number.

I don't understand how we were able to drive the truck back to the farm. The engine kept cutting and blowing black smoke out of the tail pipe. After the gas tank and fuel pump, next I removed the cylinder heads. One of the heads had a crack, so I had to go to junkyard to get a used one.

So I redid the valves, replaced gaskets, and shaved both heads. After that, I replaced the water pump, starter, alternator, and battery. That was just the beginning. None of the taillights or turn signals worked, so I rewired the back end. I replaced all sensors on the engine and ignition switch. I regretted ever buying it. I even thought about junking it or selling it as is, but I was just too deep into it. Until this day, I will never own another Chevy. On top of it all, some really good deals came along for much less money, with working AC, and that were nicer looking and more comfortable. But really I didn't deserve any better, and that I would have to accept.

So I kept going and finally made it so it would drive without dying, and the important things worked. But it was still a hunk of junk man he saw me coming. I've never owned a vehicle that needed this many parts and repairs. I ended up working on it every night for over a month. But I think having a goal was good for me. During some of this time, I acquired some sort of stomach sickness. This stomach sickness went on for many weeks. I didn't know what the cause was, but I tried everything I could get over the counter. It was causing me to lose weight. I was probably getting dehydrated. But I knew, if I would leave the farm that I would get over this sickness whatever it was, God was telling me that it was time to go home Eric knew I was restless. He offered me a mobile home he owned for very reasonable rent. He knew I probably wouldn't stay, but he was trying to make it more enticing to me. Eric was always good to me and was very happy about the progress of his chickens. Then the chickens were harvested. He did quite well, but he wouldn't tell me how well. But I knew from the inspector that this was one of his best harvests. Lisa wasn't ready to see me yet, but I was making my plans of departure. I told Eric I would go for a week, take care of business, and be back. But I knew I wasn't coming back. My life was in Toledo. It was time to start mending and rebuilding my past. The day of departure, I was anxious, not sleeping soundly. Still dark, about 5:30 a.m. I walked quietly to my truck. Eric was still sleeping, and I wanted to be gone before he stepped out of bed. So leaving his key on the coffee table under an envelope. I wanted him to find it but not right away. I was mostly packed the previous night so I made one trip out, I was on my way. By now, I knew my way around pretty good, so I knew which way I was going. I planned filling up in Cleveland, about forty minutes, then to the expressway.

By the time I made it to Cleveland, my tire was going flat at the gas station. Well, at least it was handy. I could see the leak; so I bought a plug kit, fixed it, filled up, and kept on going. The truck was far from reliable, so I was waiting for something else to happen. But it kept on running and going. Knoxville was the next destination, and that's what I hoped for, one stretch at a time. Well, it was time to eat, so I exited the expressway for a waffle house just south of Knoxville. Stepped out ready for a good breakfast, and as I was stepping out of my truck, I heard a boom followed by a loud hissing noise. What the heck. I looked over and watched my left rear tire go flat very quickly. The valve stem blew out; God was really watching out for me. This could have happened going seventy miles per hour. Well, I was hungary, so I shrugged my shouldes and went in to eat. Everyone in the restaurant heard the noise and were pering out the windows looking to see the excitement. People were friendly, and I easily received direction to the nearest tire shop. I didn't have a spare, but I did have a jack, lugwrench and a bicycle to carry the tire to the tire shop. I very awkwardly hoisted the wheel onto the handlebars and proceeded down the road a couple of miles. After a couple of hours, it was fixed, and I was back on the road. If the truck were to keep running, I could've made it to Toledo by evening. But I was in no rush so I found a motel for the night just south of Lexington, Kentucky.

I went picked up a rack of ribs and cold cokacola returned to motel to chill. It had been awhile since I'd had ribs and they were delicious.

I really didn't know what I'd do when I made it to Toledo because Lisa wasn't ready to see me yet for another week. But I had to go and my stomach issue was already getting better, so I knew I was doing the right thing. So the next night, I stayed at a different motel this time north of Lexington, Kentucky. The truck was running awful and was leaking a lot of transmission oil, so I stopped a couple of times to make repairs, then I popped a hose and overheated, but I had plenty of time to tinker with the peice of junk.

Also somewhere along the way, I lost my thirty-day tag and was driving with no plates, so I made my days short. When I made it to Toledo, I rented a motel room, then went to take care of title and plates so at least I'd be legal. I stayed in motels for four more nights. Then I couldn't spend anymore and decided it was time to camp again.

So I camped at public water access with a one-and-a-half-mile breakwater wall to Lake Erie—a woody, rocky nature trail. I'd camped there many times through the years, and fishing was okay too.

After talking to Lisa on the phone, she agreed to meet me there and hike to my camping spot. So Lisa came to meet me, and we hiked out to my spot. We had a long conversation. I did my best to explain what went on over the past five months. I also did my best to convey the changes I'd been making and would be making. I did not pressure her to let me come home, but after some conversation and warming up to each other, she asked me to come back home. There would be ground rules, which I agreed to. Lisa expected me to put my time into recovery. I would get counseling, go to a lot of meetings, and do only what was important to a full recovery. That meant no working or very little. I had a large pile of old baggage, and I didn't know how my kids would react to this. But I knew Lisa was not going back to the life I was living before, and I had fully accepted that I wasn't going back either. But I also knew that only time would convince others that my life had changed. So I had work to do, and it wouldn't be fun or easy but necessary and rewarding in the long run.

CHAPTER 10

Homecoming and Reconciliation

S O I MOVED BACK home. It felt awkward after being gone five months. I was starting over with everything. The first thing I did was to start with AA, going to at least two meetings a day. I liked going to meetings. I met a lot of people that had all kinds of problems and baggage just like me. Some had worse pasts than I, and others didn't. But we all had one thing in common, and that was the devastation caused by drugs and alcohol addictions—destroyed marriages and relationships with friends, siblings, children, and places of employment. Many people had served or were serving jail time. Many did not have driver's licenses; many for a long time. Drugs and alcohol can be the root cause for many problems of all sorts and many years of pain and destruction. At AA, we share our strength, experience, and hope. The twelve steps offer solutions to repair the wreckage of the past by making ammends to people we've injured and methods for creating an exciting, fulfilling, selfless, and better future.

So going to regular meetings was first, then I went to Harbor Behavioral Health. They set me up with a psychiatrist, a monthly counselor, and group meetings for a full year. So I did this faithfully every week, and I was also drug tested, giving Lisa peace of mind. I was clean, so it was no worry to me. During this time, I had no desire for drugs and alcohol, but my life needed a lot of repairs. So I needed to keep doing everything I could. All these meetings and counseling helped me to be on course and on target. When I was at meetings, I didn't share very often. I didn't believe I had anything to offer. I just listened, studied, prayed, and meditated.

I was very determined in my first year of recovery, but I had to keep it to myself. So being in these group meetings helped keep me from feeling completely alone. In this first year, who will believe what you say no matter how serious you are? So I didn't try. I was determined in my head and with God. God knew my true thoughts, and he helped me in many ways through these years.

So when it came time to see the psychiatrist the first time, he'd heard it all and didn't ask me many questions but diagnosed me bipolar and prescribed medication two times daily. These first few months back at home, I wasn't happy. Lisa and I were okay; it was just me. I was taking long naps in the afternoon between meetings. I was depressed about back debts, taxes, and also not being able to contribute to the household. Lisa worked very hard to support us, and she didn't want me to work. She thought it would interrupt my recovery. But I didn't feel right and told her I had to get a job, anything, but I needed to contribute. By now, I had visited my kids and grandkids; but to me, it was still about proving myself. So I didn't try hard to sell myself. That was going to be a process, and I had to be patient. It was me at fault. After being sober for more than six months, I went to temp services, filled out their questionnaires, and did their test, maybe to find a job suitable for me. Then one day, I was called for an interview. It wasn't the kind of job I had hoped for—a dirty place, unfamiliar work, but mechanical and electrical. I could learn. This was not an exciting job, but it offered good health insurance and was 100 percent paid with forty hours. In the past, this was one of Lisa's biggest concerns, so that made it important to me now. The pay wasn't great, but at least, I would be able to contribute and start paying old debts. I would change my schedule for meetings. I would need to go in the evenings. No more afternoon naps. I was still far from a happy person. I had good days, but it was still hard to be happy with an unrepaired broken past. But now I could start fixing it. So I wasn't thrilled with the new job, and I had a lot of learning to do. Also I worked through the temp agency for three months, so none of the benefits would start kicking in until I became officially hired. But I was able to start organizing my life a little. I started attending new meetings because of my schedule. I went into Michigan and started out at least three meetings a week plus two meetings with Harbor, so I stayed busy. I believed being busy was good for my recovery, and I still do.

After a few months, I was able to get rid of the Chevy S-10. That was a good day. I traded it and bought a 2000 F-150. An old truck, but I knew them and liked them. Life was gradually improving. I loved my new meetings, always looking forward and never skipping. To Lisa and me, recovery was most important, and we both took it seriously. Lisa supported me 100 percent.

CHAPTER 11

Reflection

EEING WHERE I AM at today, sometimes I look back to my past, attempting to make sense of it all. In one hand, it doesn't make sense; and in the other, it makes complete sense. I was raised in a Christian home. I attended Sunday school regularly. There were many great mentors in my life. My parents never smoked, drank, or swore. How was it I went down the path I did? Many examples of happy, prosperous, moral futures were visible to me. Sure, my parents, family, and mentors weren't perfect; but who is? I don't have all the answers to these questions. When I look back, I don't understand why I did the things I did. Was all this predestined for a bigger purpose? Maybe. Sometimes we have to make the best of circumstances we've created. I do my best to explain and rationalize some of these questions, but the rest only God knows. I believe a lot of it started with embarrassment, envy, and circumstances out of my control. I was embarrassed I had to go to church so much, often wearing clothes handed down by five older brothers. We drove rusty, beat-up old cars, many without heat while other people had descent, modern, comfortable auto mobiles. I wasn't one of the popular kids partly because we were never in style. I know now how unimportant these things are, but back then, I didn't understand. I only knew how it made me feel. Mom and Dad were not materialistic; things were not very important for the most part. We didn't have a pool or air-conditioning or color TV or a riding lawnmower for our large yard. We also were not given allowance or any money from our parents. As I aged, I desired fun toys or doing things that only money would pay for. I had friends in the same boat. So we found things to do, or we learned to acquire what we desired many times dishonestly. In no way am I trying to excuse my actions. So after I had a falling out with my parents, I found it easier to follow my selfish desires. I still believed in morality, but I found ways to rationalize bad behavior. Then after my accident at twelve—a physical affliction I was born with—and with influence of my friends, drugs and alcohol seeped into my world. So by the time I turned fifteen, love of money, my selfish desires, drugs, alcohol, a hunger for excitement, and adventure controlled my being. By the time I was seventeen, I was a blossoming alcoholic with a love for drugs and money. I was also a thrill seeker, so I needed money to keep it all alive with big plans and dreams for the future.

But still, by the time I was in my midtwenties, there were enough indicators in my life that the existence of one Creator was undeniable to me. Having a relationship with that Creator is difficult when you worship money and materialism. But I was not about to change my ways because I was having too much fun, I thought. When I married and raised a family, some things changed, but my materialistic goals just became bigger. Life was better superficially but only temporarily. I would ask God to protect and bless my family, and he did exponentially despite my reckless behavior. But eventually God allowed me to suffer the consequences I had created. But sadly my wife and family also suffered too.

But God stuck with me and protected me during my learning years. God took my bad judgments and made good of them. He is now giving me an opportunity to use my past mistakes and shortcomings to possibly help others. God has blessed me by his grace so I can bless others. My past now becomes a tool. During my troubled years, God blessed me and my family despite my shortcomings, but he also left me to my own devices. During my troubled years, there were times of repentance and forgiveness and times when he still spoke to me. These times were few and far between, but when it happened, it would always strengthen my faith in him.

There was this time in the middle of the day, a few years after my father had passed away. My mother was still grieving her loss and was lonely and really missed her past. God spoke to me through the Holy Spirit, telling me to send her a card and tell her how much she meant to me and what a wonderful mother she had been and how much I loved her. This came to me instantly just as clear as day. I was a selfish, insensitive, unemotional individual; so there was no way it was my idea.

I answered God and said, *Yes, I'll do it right away.*

That day, I picked up a nice card and sent it the next morning. Mom was so thrilled; it made her week. It was just the pick-me-up she needed that day. She put it up so she could read it over and over when she needed to. This was completely out of character for me. But I did as God instructed me, and he gave me the words to write. This day, that card meant more than words could express. This was just one time I realized how important it could be to follow his instructions. Sometimes when I was alone thinking about the power of my addictions and how I was unable to stop on my own, in the back of my mind, I knew that God would remove my obsession with drugs, alcohol, and other things if I would ask him sincerely and mean it; but I just wasn't willing to give up what had become my idols. I didn't think I could be happy. I was so deceived and misguided by the evil one. I wasn't ready to change and totally trust God until I was fifty-five years old. I think how many years I wasted and how much better a husband, father, friend, brother, and son I could have been. Well, I can't change the past, but I can change today and hopefully tomorrow. Life, character, and actions don't change overnight; but every day I get up and do my best to be a better person and ask God for wisdom and direction to know the knowledge of his will. So today, I work extra hard. God gives me energy, will, drive, enthusiasm, and strength; and I give him all the glory.

In my first six months of sobriety, I didn't recognize God speaking to me always. But I knew he was with me every minute of the day preparing a path for me, and he was always faithful. This one particular day, my mind was very troubled. I had really messed up my life. At this point, I was homeless, over five hundred miles from my home. I wasn't happy and had no idea what to do, and it seemed my future was doomed. By God's grace, I had shed my destructive addictions; but after forty years of this lifestyle, I was lost. My body didn't understand. God was allowing me to wander in the wilderness, and this day, he spoke to me.

Instantly a mass of words flowed into my head. It was too much for me to remember, so I grabbed my notepad and wrote as fast as I could. This was not of me, and I knew that. These are the exact words I wrote that day:

> I choose to be happy.
> I choose not to be angry.
> I choose not to be depressed.
> I choose not to be bitter.
> I choose not to dwell on the past.
> I choose to look for the good in all people.
> I choose to have a positive future.
> I choose to make sound decisions.
> I choose to work hard and manage my finances responsibly.
> I choose not to feel guilty about the decisions made today.
> I will practice my faith the way that God chooses for me, and God will choose my destiny.
> I will do what I can to help other addicts.
> I will love well and have fun.
> I will enjoy my family, my friends, sports, music, fishing, and my hobbies.

These are the things I believe in. Words are exactly as delivered that day. I consider this a covenant between God and me. These things can't come true if I choose to not follow God's will. But this gave me a map, a standard, a plan, and a direction to follow. I do my best to keep my covenant with God. God has helped me to achieve these promises and much more than I could've ever imagined. Ninety-nine percent of these promises are true today. I don't have to look at this list daily to check them off. As I stayed on track with recovery, these things came true. It took time, years; but along with patience, long suffering, and the grace of God, all is possible.

CHAPTER 12

Proving Change

T HE FIRST YEAR OF recovery was not easy and not very fun. I had my good days, and meetings were essential. I showed up to meetings always on time, but I never shared with the group. First I was scared, and second I didn't believe I had anything worthwhile to offer. After all, I was a loser. Who wanted to hear what I had to say? Also I had no sponsor yet. Lisa would question me. I would say I was being careful and assured her I would find one in due time. By late in my first year, I started seeing a psychiatrist, and he started me on medication, diagnosing me as bipolar with depression. I was depressed, and I had lots of good reasons to be. I had a very difficult time having a positive attitude. I was contributing now, but that wasn't nearly enough by my standards. I felt I had a lot of making up for the past to do. I couldn't let go of the past. I tried, but it was too close to my heart. Now I had been seeing my kids and grandkids from time to time, but they were guarded understandably. No one knew what to think. My family all wanted the best, but the only thing to prove true was time. I went on some small one-nighter fishing trips, and they were okay. I loved driving and fishing, but it was difficult to feel any real joy in that first year. Working and going to meetings, as many as possible, were the only things that really helped me.

I would love to say that, when God removed my obsession for drugs and alcohol, life all became wonderful; but that was just not how it happened. It took over forty years to get where I ended up, and it couldn't get fixed in a year. A full recovery takes time, work, prayer, love of family, and as much help as I could get from outside sources. God was with me always during my recovery, but there was much I needed to learn, mostly about myself. Some of my most valuable help in recovery was AA and the people in AA. The nuts and bolts of AA is the Twelve-Step Program. Now the Twelve Steps can be useful to anyone. One doesn't have to be an alcoholic to benefit from them. The Twelve Steps are based on biblical teachings and very useful to anyone. During my first year, I studied the Twelve Steps, read the Big Book, but didn't do the steps with a sponsor.

But I know I did the first three steps while in detox. I didn't even know what the steps were, but automatically I just knew what was needed. I was on my knees several times a day. I asked God to remove my obsessions because I couldn't do it on my own. I asked God to forgive my sins and told him I would follow his will from now on. I was very serious in my prayers. I was ready for a new life. I was tired and guilty about the hurt that I had inflicted upon my wife and kids.

I was going to change with God's help no matter what it would take. During the first year, I needed to keep reminding myself of my promise to myself and God. I really couldn't say a whole lot about my promises and plans to my family.

What good would it do to make promises to my wife and family? I believed my words, for the most part, were empty. Only time could prove my true intentions. The only thing I would say was that I'd keep working and go to meetings, my doctors, and treatment, which I did without fail. So a lot of what I did the first couple of years was only discussed with God or other group members. I was very intent on proving myself then and now, but I will prove by my actions, not empty words. I kept working on my relationship with my Savior, which I will continue until my last day on earth. God is my strength.

So my first year sober wasn't really much fun. It was work and about proving myself. Most people don't understand the realities of alcoholism. But another alcoholic does. This is why recovering alcoholics and addicts can become the most powerful counselors and mentors to other alcoholics. Most average people can't understand why an alcoholic doesn't use their willpower to stop drinking or control their drinking, but alcoholism is a disease. The first year of recovery especially requires help as much as possible, not just physical but mental and spiritual. When in my first year, there was an emptiness that could not be filled. That emptiness brought lack of joy, depression, anxiety, frustration, and boredom. This is why help is so important, or alcohol will suck you back into oblivion. The most powerful antidote is God. This can be extremely difficult for many to accept this concept; but it is essential and will bring full recovery, a boundless joy, prosperity, and so much more.

CHAPTER 13

Validation

MY SECOND YEAR OF recovery was much like the first year. I was attending AA meetings three times a week and group therapy with Harbor. I had adjusted pretty well to my new job, still a dirty place with many health hazards but steady work and decent benefits. I tried my best to be busy all day and most evenings. This helped keep my mind off my issues. The correct combination and dosage of my medications for bipolar condition are difficult to find. So I had issues with cloudiness in my head, just had a hard time adjusting, and was drowsy, cloudy, and still depressed. Life had many improvements, but life still didn't have the joy and excitement I desired. But I still wasn't deserving of any of this. I was working on my debts one at a time with help from family. I was still waiting for an agreement with the IRS. During this time, I had made another appointment with my medical doctor. I found I was getting out of breath tying my boot laces, and I tired easily. So I went in for a full physical, thinking my lungs were the problem. I was not expecting the news coming at me. The first test they did after the preliminaries was an EKG. I thought my heart was great until they told me I might have a problem. The doctor said sometimes an EKG could be incorrect, so they referred me to a cardiologist for further testing. This was a real blow, but it shouldn't have been, considering all the years of abuse to my body. For many years, I drank beer all day, took painkillers, and ate everything bad.

I didn't care much for fruit and vegetables, but I loved meat, all meat—fat didn't matter. I had a terrible diet for many years. Toward the end of my drinking years, I didn't even eat much. I just filled myself with beer.

I would wash the pills down with beer, and that would allow me to work twice as hard for more hours. So I was abusing my heart big-time, not really caring but not really thinking I was hurting myself. After all, I was born healthy, never sick except hangovers. I worked very hard for over forty years. So it shouldn't have been a shock to hear I had serious heart problems, but it was. So I went to a cardiologist and went for an echogram.

After that test meeting with the cardiologist, he informed me I had had a heart attack and had a weak heart muscle. This meant the heart pump volume was very low. Well, this explained my breathing problem. This was one and one-half years after becoming clean and sober. This didn't seem fair, but this was the consequences of a bad, unhealthy lifestyle. So next they put me on high doses of several different heart medications. Now I would be taking so many different medications it would be difficult to keep track of. I bought a pill organizer to take what I needed at the right times. Here I was doing my best to be off all drugs and forced to take handfuls twice daily. But I did exactly what was prescribed, hoping for some improvement later. They set me up with another appointment in three months. So I went back after three months for a checkup for more bad news.

When I went for the next appointment, they believed I was not improving, then increased my dosage so high that, after a week, I was having hallucinations. So they set an appointment date for about four months to see an electrocardiologist. I was to have one more test on my heart and be set up for a defibrillator, basically a pacemaker purposed differently. This really scared me. Fifty-seven years old with a pacemaker. I was beside myself. Now during these times, I prayed daily and read my Scripture. My faith in God was powerful, and I worked hard every day to strengthen my relationship with God to live a God-centered life and believed he would bring me through this to finish his work and build relationships. I can't do that if I'm dead, and I did not want to burden anyone to take care of me. So I was willing to do whatever I had to do. Well, a little before the time of the final test to decide on pacemaker, I made an appointment with my general doctor. I liked my doctor and had been with him a long time and trusted him implicitly. So he received all my results from the cardiologist, and we met. Then he told me that I could reverse my condition. I was all ears, but it certainly wasn't an easy alternative.

Then he proceeded, saying, "Change your lifestyle, the way you eat, and the way you live."

I had thought I was doing everything good, but I had a lot to learn. My doctor spent a full hour explaining many things to me. It would be very difficult for me to do. But life was precious, and I didn't like drugs anymore and would do just about anything to get away from them.

Then he said, "No meat. No dairy. Nothing from an animal."

This was my diet. I loved cheese, pork, hamburgers, ribs, and wings. I had not changed my eating after getting sober. If anything, I was eating worse. I had gained twenty-five pounds and believed I was now healthy. The doctor didn't agree, wanting me to lose weight and basically go vegan. You got to be kidding. I made fun of vegans. I thought vegans were goofy, and I didn't want to be one. The price was too high though. I had to change. Once I decide to do something, I try to do it right. I assured the doctor I would do my best, and he wanted to see me back in three months.

The next day, I went out and bought the most powerful blender I could get. Lisa and I went grocery shopping, buying fruits, vegetables, and healthy ingredients. Starting out not knowing what I was doing was a learning process. The doctor told me it would be a journey and take time to adjust. The doctor was right; it was and still is. I made two large smoothies for every day. I didn't like eating fruits and vegetables. I still don't, so I forced myself to drink them. I still didn't switch over all the way, but my eating greatly improved. I made some gross smoothies. It took a while to learn the right combinations, also causing gas and stomach issues, but I stuck to it. I wanted to be healthier and heal the heart and other organs. Then after a couple of months, I went to see the cardiologist for a final test and diagnosis before pacemaker.

The last test was a MUGA scan, and it took about forty minutes. After the results, there was a meeting with the cardiologist. I was told this test came back about twenty percent better than the last test. Wow, this was great news. The pacemaker would be canceled for now. God was working on my behalf. This excited and motivated me to work harder. Next I met again with my medical doctor and did a blood test so now he could show me where I needed improvement. This appointment was also positive, I had lost seven pounds and my blood pressure had decreased. After this appointment, I would visit my medical doctor every three months, and I still do. Month after month, I had streamlined my diet. When I'd see my doctor, he would cut more out and correct my mistakes. I also started taking karate. My energy level was improving as the months went on. I did my best to always be physically active and stuck to the diet. I no longer get out of breath easily. One by one, the doctor weaned me off the medication. Today I take no medication except for my mental condition, which is so effective I won't even think of stopping for now. The doctor told me there was no way I could be as active as I am if my heart wasn't pumping adequately. God is good, and I give him all the glory. I don't know if I am completely out of the woods with my heart, but I will keep doing what I'm doing. My overall health for my age is great, and I work hard to keep it that way.

So toward the end of my second year of sobriety, things were slowly getting better. With much help from family, I was getting my debts under control. I had a long-term agreement set up with the IRS. The payment to the IRS was about a car payment, so I had to accept having to drive my old truck for quite a few more years. But that's okay because I don't deserve to own a nice truck until I have paid my dues. Also, I started feeling better in many ways. No more pit in my stomach. I have lost that empty feeling. After many years of physical abuse and gluttony, it took me almost two years to get over it. But I really felt good—more energy and more ambition. All the things I believed would be gone forever. I really thought I couldn't be happy or cope with life without those addictions. The second year was when I really realized just how mistaken I had been. My head was clear; my memory was improving. I was content with myself. This didn't mean life was perfect. I still had good days and bad days. Now I was developing the tools to cope with ups and downs and be happy and content. I had peace about my life, and I was slowly building my trust back with my family. You know, with many years of causing mistrust, it can't just be earned overnight. Most people will forgive, but that doesn't mean they forget the hurt and emotional discomfort you may have put them through. I didn't understand this completely and knew this would take time, maybe a long time. I hope God will give me adequate time to prove that I am trustworthy and to live the life that God would choose me to live.

The road to recovery from forty years is a long road. It takes time, work, and perseverance; but it is well worth it. So I surrounded myself with good people. Most of the people were just like me, some less and some more, but the basic problem is still the same. We all had to admit we were powerless over alcohol. We found a way to never have to pick up that first drink. So I was invested going to several meetings weekly.

One night, at the end of the meeting, a good friend named Grant walked over to speak with me.

Grant said, "I noticed you don't share very much with our group."

I responded, saying, "I don't think I have much to offer. My life is a mess."

Grant said, "You know, I think you have much to offer, and I think you can help others with your story."

I knew Grant was correct; and I admitted that and said, "Yeah, you're right. I'm going to do better."

Grant really started me thinking, but I had a hard time. I was scared. When I talked, I would stumble. But that night, I decided it was time to get out of myself and start opening up. I knew it was also important to insure long-term sobriety, and it is also my responsibility to help the newcomers as much as I possibly can. So I did, I began to share what I could at every meeting. Sometimes just a little, but I did my best to contribute at every meeting I attended. When I was asked to moderate, I did it even though I was scared and wanted to say no. But I found that it really did help me and allowed me feel better about myself. I would stumble, sometimes be at a loss for words, but I realized that this also helped the newcomer to be more comfortable to also be open and share. By the end of my second year of sobriety, my life did get better.

CHAPTER 14

Awakening

THE THIRD YEAR WAS when my life really started to become full circle. But I still hadn't done the AA Twelve Steps, and I still hadn't chosen a sponsor. Even though I hadn't done the steps, God's promises to me were being fulfilled. I fully intended doing the AA responsibilities, and it was weighing on my mind. Prayer was a big part of my life, studying the Scripture and reading as many good books as possible. Now I knew God has plans for me but was still at a loss of purpose. He is preparing me for something. With the anticipation of my future, I was full of new energy, motivation, and ambition. My workdays flew by. My head was clear, and I believed I was wiser than I had ever been. Most of my feelings, I still kept between God and me as I was still building trust and credibility. The big difference in my life was that I had become a man of God. I still had a lot to learn and much to prepare for on the horizon. I chose to follow God's will and not my own. So my third year of sobriety became very spiritual. I prayed continually throughout the day and walked with the Lord to the best of my ability. I prayed for my family, direction, wisdom, a heart to hear, and the knowledge of his will. About this time, I became very compelled to make a road trip and planned pretty well. I had done very little traveling on my own since coming home, mainly because I really didn't enjoy it that much. The objective was to scope out fishing and lodging accommodations with my sons and son-in-law. I decided on Wisconsin. I had never been there. I figured there would be good fishing.

While searching the map, I was drawn toward the northwestern tip bordering Lake Superior. There are a group of islands called the Apostle Islands. That intrigued me. It looked appealing. I decided it was the perfect place for prayer and meditation. So this was definitely the main goal of the trip. I left Toledo in the middle of the afternoon so as to drive through the night. I've always enjoyed night driving—less traffic and easier on my eyes. This way, I could drive until I became tired I'd look for a rest area pull in, sleep in my back seat. Well, I made it a good distance into Wisconsin, and I had driven until about 2:30 AM. I awoke about 7:00 AM and continued North.

It was a beautiful morning, sunny, and comfortable temperature. I loved Wisconsin instantly, what a beautiful state the scenery was breathtaking, a lot like Michigan which I also love. So I drove on appreciating God's majestic creations. As I traveled North toward the apostle islands, I stopped in several small towns, checked out lakes, rivers, streams, and parks. So far, Wisconsin proved to be a sportsmans paradise. But I didn't stop long, I just kept driving, excited to see Lake Superior. As I was traveling along the lake, I came to a town called Washburn, a very neat patriotic town with veteran memorials and rows of flags. My kind of town.

I stopped near a marina to admire the water and hundreds of sailboats. After admiring the wonderful scenery a bit, I kept going toward my destination. As I got close, I began looking for parks to fulfill my vision with a picnic table overlooking lake superior. This part of the drive was quite enjoyable, very secluded, lots of trees, and foliage on a smooth hilly two-lane highway, then I came to a public park, drove back in, and was disappointed to find it packed, not even a place to park; but people seemed to be enjoying. Boats, jet skis, tents, and campers everywhere. Apparently, people of Wisconsin love the outdoor water life. But this was not what I wanted, so I kept driving.

So I drove. It seemed there was nothing, then I came to another park. This was the same as the other park, packed and people having fun. So I drove again, found a gas stop, got a Coke, and drove some more. I was starting to think I wouldn't find what I was looking for. Then I came to a roadside rest and pulled in. Only one car, no one to be seen on the lake, and there was one picnic table empty on the lake with a cliff overlooking. This was almost exactly what I visualized. I was meant to be here. This was a divine appointment. I was no longer a believer of coincidence. Things happen for a reason, and I was about to find out the reason. I parked and quickly grabbed my Bible and headed for the table.

After admiring the scenery and serenity, I thought it was time to open the Bible. But before that, I prayed, thanking God for safe travel, the opportunity to be here, and what he would have me hear. As I opened it, a wind came up and blew the pages until I stopped them. That was the sign of what to read. I started at John chapter 7, verse 14, titled "Jesus Teaches at the Feast":

> Not until halfway through the feast did Jesus go up to the temple courts and begin to teach. The Jews were amazed and asked how did this man get so much learning without having studied? Jesus answered it comes from him who sent me. If anyone chooses to do God's will, he will find out whether my teaching comes from God or whether I speak on my own. He who speaks on his own does so to gain honor for himself, but he who works for the honor of the one who sent him is a man of truth. There is nothing false about him.

Reading this was just the beginning of what was about to happen to me this weekend. I read the passage through several times, then continued to read as I meditated on the words. At this point, I did not know what the Lord was telling me. More would be revealed later, but I knew it was significant to my future. This passage and its relevance becomes clearer, which I will come back to later. God can be mysterious, but that is what makes pursuing and following so exciting to me.

So after thinking on this experience for a bit, I decided it was time to drive on. As I drove, I realized I was at complete peace and contentment with all my present circumstances. This short trip was bringing spiritual depth of exponential proportion into my heart and soul. Just three years prior, I had left my addictions behind me, leaving an emptiness in my stomach and a hole in my psychological being. I was sober but didn't think that I could ever be happy again without drugs, alcohol, and a ton of money. I really did not know what happiness is anymore. But I now realized that I was happy, content and truly enjoying myself again. I had been doing all I could to repair the past, but that alone does not bring happiness.

While feeling this contentment was when God really started talking to me. God first reminded me of his promises to me and reassured me that I was following his will. While being encouraged and inspired, I kept driving up to Minnesota; and as I entered Duluth, my brakes started grinding. I was thoroughly enjoying God's presence with me. I didn't want to stop but needed to remedy the situation. So I headed south in Minnesota, now looking for an auto parts store. It was getting late when I came to a small town, and their parts store was closed. The brakes were grinding metal to metal, so I needed to stop for the night. I stopped at a rest area and slept in the back seat. First thing in the morning, I drove to the nearest town and located an O'Reilly.

I had brought tools, heavy-duty jack, and jack stands. So there in the parking lot, I jacked it up and installed new brake pads on the front. Less than one hour, I was back on the road, figuring it was time to gradually go toward home. I still felt the same peace and joy of the previous day; the brakes were just a slight glitch. God took up right where we left off, encouraging and inspiring me. As I drove, the interaction became more intense and more clear. Now this is not the first time I recognized God speaking to me, but it is still one of the most monumental to me. He instructed me of the steps that he wanted me to do next and that he would instruct me further of the steps after they were completed. He would give me time to ponder, but I felt his presence with me. I barely stopped for anything that day because I didn't want anything to interfere with this spiritual time. He instructed me of the tools I would need and the things that I needed to take care of. God was revealing some of my future to me, not everything, but enough to know my life was meant to have much more meaning than I ever thought could be possible and that I would have ambition, drive, and passion but it would be for him. My life was about to be much different than I had ever imagined. Not only was God speaking to me, but he was also answering my questions.

First was to get a sponsor, do the Twelve Steps and become more involved with AA, and to step out of my comfort zone.

Then I needed to become much more knowledgeable about the Scripture. Now I thought I knew the Bible well. I had read it several times. But my need would require me to know it much better using all methods available and spend much more time studying. This weekend was a powerful filling of the Holy Spirit. God was assuring me I had been doing the right things for the past three years, yet there was much more to do as preparation for much more. Most of this still stays between God and I but by midnight my head was about to burst. So much information and spiritual blessing within such a short amount of time. So I made an agreement that I would stop, get some sleep, and continue driving as soon as I awoke.

I awoke, hopped back into the drivers seat, and started driving. As soon as I resumed highway speed everything from the previous day flowed back into my head and God's presence was just as strong. Now there was no doubts as to what had transpired. So I thanked God and agreed I to do my best to follow his will. All of these changes have been completely out of character for me. I have always been a selfish, greedy, strong-willed proud person, and it only became worse with time and addictions. I had always planned and predicted my own future so this was so new to me. I am sure with God on my side, this future will be much better and sure to happen.

To sum it all up, God instructed me that I had work to do. I needed to get my life in order. I needed to work on my inner being;

to live as Jesus would want me to live; to be loving, kind, and gentle; to live for others rather than myself; to know and understand the Scripture so that I may use it to the best of my abilities to help others; to free myself of all material obstacles in my life; and to be willing to go and do as God calls me. Only God could do this for me. I do not possess these qualities on my own. The power of God is amazing, the way he can change and renew a person if only that person is willing. This encounter was life-changing for me, it only deepened my desire to have a closer relationship with Jesus Christ. By noon that day, all that needed to be said had been said.

As I completed the remainder of my trip, I felt an overwhelming sense of peace, joy, and the presence of God. Now the vision was clear to me, so I knew what I must do.

After I made it home, I only told a few close people about my experience, but it was everything to me. At the very next AA meeting, I chose a sponsor, and he accepted to do the Twelve Steps with me. We started a meeting the next week to work through the steps. Whatever it was I did, I did to the best of my ability, including my job. I had always done pretty well on the job; but I improved my attitude, stopped complaining, and gave all jobs 100 percent of my abilities. When jobs became more than my knowledge allowed, I would study, research, and figure out how to get it done and then double- and triple-check my quality. I started to step out of my comfort zone and do things I wouldn't normally do. But the things that I did added to character, knowledge, and humility. I tried to do more for others, expecting nothing in return. I also spent more time reading, books of history, famous evangelists, spiritual books, and books to increase my general knowledge to help with the plans God has for me. Knowledge and wisdom became important to me; Holy Spirit would help point out the books to be helpful, and I read them using discernment, using an open mind but always backing my final beliefs with scripture. My days and weeks were very full with reading, writing, praying, going to meetings, and doing my best to put family first. The busyness was fulfilling, and I was and still am excited about every new day. Shortly, after getting a sponsor, I became a sponsor. Sponsoring is just as rewarding as being sponsored, maybe more.

It's pretty cool how things work out and come together. I no longer believe in coincidence or luck all things happen for a reason, God knows what he's doing. I also took up karate, something I've always wanted to do but other things got in the way. I became more serious about my personal health, stayed active, and eat and drink healthy. It's hard to be perfect. There is always give-and-take, but persistence and consistency pay off.

The instructions were clear; my motivation, drive, and passion to do good were at full speed. The third year of sobriety was when I really awoke and realized just how great life is. Now it isn't great just because I'm sober. What's great is becoming the person I could have been now, ridding the obstacles hindering that growth. No matter where I'm at or what the circumstance or environment are, I'm at peace. I have no resentments or bitterness toward any person or entity. The harmful obsessions I once had are gone. I have a quality of life no matter what I'm doing. I am optimistic. I almost never have to take days from work from sickness, hangovers, or lame excuses, only planned days to enjoy life and maybe work at home. I now get pleasure from doing things I would never do before because my way of thinking has completely changed. Also as the result of three years of no drugs, no alcohol, and living on mostly fruits and vegetables, my mind and memory have increased incredibly. I now concentrate on learning as much as possible every day. While I was consumed, I really didn't enjoy eating that much. It was just a chore to get it over with. Eat as fast as possible only because it was a necessity, not enjoyment. Now I only have a hamburger about once a month, but I savor every bite or a good lobster now and then. My taste buds are incredible. And family is a treat. I love my family and value every minute I can spend with them.

And I've found great true friends that I also cherish my time with. When I was consumed, I just wanted to be by myself. I didn't need anyone. What a sad existence. Harmful addictions are powerful thieves. They rob you of life, happiness, and financial security, then leave a path of destruction. Worry is an emotion which consumes many people, including me. But that is something else that has changed for me. I now worry very little, hardly at all. Sure, I have concerns and things I don't like; but at the end of the day, God takes care of everything. If I have standards and guidelines and try to live as Jesus would to the best of my abilities, there just isn't much to worry about. Things will happen and do happen, but God is with me to help navigate me through rough waters. I still enjoy a lot of what I used to enjoy—the great outdoors, travel, music, building, household work, and my job. No need for worry. All will work out one way or another. God knows what I enjoy the most, and he will present those opportunities. But most of all, I choose to follow God's will, which gives me peace and joy; and much good comes from that.

Also, my health has increased greatly with energy, strength, and stamina. My cognitive health has also improved with much clearer thinking and memory and my drive for intellectual stimulation. I have a great desire for learning. I believe I'm never too old to learn. I see several doctors on a regular basis, doing my best to follow recommendations.

Many years of extreme abuse to my body did damage, which is not repairable or reversible. I did the damage, so it's something I accept and live with. And I can't expect God to heal me from self-inflicted damage.

But if I'd have kept going the way I was, I'd probably be either dead or a vegetable in a nursing home from a whole host of different reasons. But I am alive; full of life, ambition, and exuberance; and living a quality, clean life, hopefully for many more good years (God willing). Also, with attendance in alcoholics (anonymous), I've become much more involved sharing, moderating, giving leads, and reaching out to other struggling alcoholics and addicts. This was not natural for me being that I had become an introvert, but doing these activities helped to lighten my burdens and guilt from the past. It is still difficult for me to put into words the psychological and spiritual changes that have come over me throught these experiences.

What is the most difficult is why it took so long to see the light while it was right in front of my face. Drugs, alcohol, and the pursuit of money had a terrible negative effect on my mind, causing me to believe what wasn't at all true. I really believed these things were what would bring true happiness. How deceived and warped I had become and how thankful I am for God's grace. Also my wife, Lisa; my kids; and family were used as God's instruments to initiate and encourage my recovery. Coming out of the abyss and realizing how much valuable time was wasted will always hurt me knowing how it could've been.

Also I dishonored my good name, a name that my family built before me while I squandered the reputation of that name. The things that became important to me when my eyes were opened. I can never fully make up for the dishonor and mistakes in my past, that's just something I must live with for the rest of my days. I have also harmed many others in those years of depravity, people I may never see again that I have influenced or damaged in some way. If only there were a way to explain this to the many people in a state of depravity with no apparent way out, or don't even understand how much better life could be. There are millions of people throughout the world that are trapped in their circumstance. For me during my third year of sobriety, God awakened me to the realities of the past and the present and the glory and the majesty of a living, personal, and powerful God today.

There is so much for mankind to experience if only they seek, find, and follow. It took me well over forty years to awake. The miracle of salvation can be difficult to explain to the unbeliever, but the believer can fully understand. Three years is still young in sobriety, and there was much to learn. But as sobriety increases, so does knowledge and understanding of the disease. Alcoholics and addicts still need to live one day at a time. They need to meet with other recovering addicts and also continue with wise, experienced counsel.

CHAPTER 15

The Beginning

APRIL 1, 2016, THE day I walked out into the sunlight, leaving Arrowhead Behavioral Health from a week of detoxification. That week was what marked a new beginning. As I looked into the sunlight, I knew my life was about to change in a very big way. At this point, I knew very little about just how much and what those changes would be. Now in my fourth year of sobriety and turning sixty, my life was still just beginning. I know a little more what those changes are now. But God will lead, and I will follow wherever he leads me.

Now being sober more than four years is huge. Being part of AA is huge. Holding a job is huge. Having a great relationship with my wife, kids, and grandkids is huge. Many great things have happened being sober, but the greatest is having a relationship with Jesus Christ. All of these other huge things are because of him. Each new year is a new beginning; and I'm excited about what God has in store for me, my family, my friends, and AA.

Just before my fourth-year anniversary, I got a message from God through a scripture reading, Matthew chapter 3, verses 13–15:

> Then Jesus came from Galilee to the Jordan to be baptized by John. But John tried to deter him saying, I need to be baptized by you, and do you come to me? Jesus replied, let it be so now; it is proper for us to do this to fulfill all righteousness. Then John consented.

As I read that scripture, I became strongly convicted, and then it became apparent it was now urgent that I be baptized. I had not been thinking about baptism for a long time, and I had rationalized that it wasn't really important, and it wouldn't keep me from heaven. While it may not keep me from heaven, it is certainly important for a believer in Christ. I realized it is an act of obedience, and it signifies Jesus dying on the cross to save me from my sins as he arose, saving me with his blood.

The very next day, I called my pastor and set up a time to meet with him. I told my pastor my story and the reason to be baptized. We set the date. I came in later in the week to tell my testimony on video. March 8, 2020, I was baptized; and my testimony was shown on video for the congregation. As I submerged underwater and came back up, I left my sins and old self behind. The pastor's sermon after my testimony was his testimony, something he hadn't done for a long time. It was a very powerful sermon. It came deep from the heart, very moving. The Spirit of God filled the sanctuary that morning. It just showed me again how very important it is to follow God's instructions. This was the last church service for months due to COVID-19. The urgency of this obedience to God was very apparent and further strengthened my faith and filled me with the Holy Spirit.

So being baptized was just another of many amazing spiritual experiences. If I had ignored the prompting of the Holy Spirit, God's blessings would pass me by and also the congregation and others moved that day.

We didn't know it would be the last church service for a long stretch, but God did. This was a great way to start my fifth year of sobriety and continue my spiritual journey.

After that day, COVID-19 changed life for most people and turned the church upside down. COVID disrupted many of my plans. My hours at work were reduced. Things I did were canceled as for many. I made the best of my time writing and working on a garden and many things around the house. I am concerned about drug and alcohol use increasing now with AA also closed for a while. All of our freedoms compromised, what will happen to this great country? Well, I am at peace with little worry knowing that God is in control. During this time, I was able to slow down a little, pray, meditate, read, and decide how to plan our future.

So after being sober four and one-half years, questions might be, Do you miss the fun of drinking and recreational drug use? Do you miss buying lottery tickets and gambling for money? Do you miss going to bars, clubs, and other party places? Do you miss doing what you want whenever you please no matter who is affected? Do you miss driving with a beer in your hand? Do you miss spending lots of money however you please? Do you miss working seventy to eighty hours per week? Do you miss going to jail? Do you miss being the life of the party, saying a lot of things you don't remember the next day? Do you miss driving fast, breaking laws, and risking life of self or others? I could go on and on, but that's not necessary to make the point.

Of course, there are fun things in my past, and they will always be. But if I could go back and do it differently, I definitely would, like most people. My biggest regret is not putting God first. I still could have had just as much fun; I believe more. My life could have had so much more meaning and could have made much better friendships. I'd have been much wiser, smarter, more respected, and more trusted and believed.

But I can't change the past. I have today and maybe tomorrow. I work every day now to build what I didn't. God is most important. Following God protects and blesses my wife and family, my church, AA, my friends, and all other people who are important. My life now has meaning; our futures are bright. I am not afraid of danger, risk, and bumps in life. I know where I'm going. My risks are thought out with a clear mind. I will still do risky and adventurous and exciting things. God knows my heart and I believe he still wants me to have fun.

God knows what I enjoy, what excites me, and what gets my adrenaline going better than I do. I don't need artificial excitement with a dead end and eternity in hell. The God who created me will supply all the excitement I can handle. I should probably be careful what I ask him for because he does answer prayer. So I won't write of my future plans because it is not up to me. But I do know that God will fulfill my desires if I follow his will and not mine. So who says you can't start life at sixty years of age? Because I'm just getting started.

EPILOGUE

P EACE SURPASSES ALL UNDERSTANDING. There is but one way to achieve this magnitude of peace and understanding. This one way comes from the grace of God. Eternity in heaven is a free gift, but we must be willing to accept this gift. It is free, so it can't be bought or earned but by the grace of God. There is one qualification. You must believe that Jesus Christ died on the cross to save us from our sins, repent, and accept him into your heart. Life will change after receiving Christ if you truly believe and follow him. I believe there is one question before making this step of faith. This question is an age-old question. This question has been a subject of controversy for thousands of years. There have been countless arguments, theories, beliefs, and disbeliefs. Science has been used to warp, confuse, and manipulate this subject. Many and all kinds of people have struggled with this question. The answer and decisions derived from our choice will completely shape our lives, future, and eternity. This is a question every human being must answer and that chooses their destiny. Yet many people do not take it seriously at all. They just go on with their lives, believing there is always a tomorrow.

The question is: Is there a God? Or is there not? It really is a loaded question, but the answer is absolutely clear if thoroughly investigated.

If there isn't a God

- If there is no God, then we are nothing. Life means nothing. We return to nothing. We die. Our body rots and turns to dirt.
- If there is no God, then there is no right and no wrong because there is nothing to base them on.
- If there is no God, then there is no truth because it can be twisted, spun, and manipulated to the ideals of the beholder.
- If there is no God, there are no true laws or moral standards, just brutal tyrants and evil dictators.
- If there is no God, there can be no true joy. Forgiveness does not exist. There is no love. There is no true justice. We are just animals only concerned with self-preservation, self-satisfaction, survival, power at any cost with no limitations, there is just self-desire, self-will, hate, and destruction.

Modern science would have you believe that, billions of years ago, there was an explosion in a black swamp somewhere. Not sure what caused the explosion or how the swamp got there. From that explosion, it miraculously caused a primitive life-form.

This life-form eventually turned into monkeys. These monkeys eventually turned into humans. I'm not sure where the other animals came from, but I'm sure there's a theory for that. Now these primitive humans evolved into a super race with power over the planet due to the increase of intelligence. And as part of the amazing reproductive system just magically came into existence. All animals, mammals, reptiles, fish, insects, plants, and all life-form could reproduce itself. All these amazing things came from an amoeba in a black swamp somewhere. I wonder what humans and animals will evolve into next.

To me, this completely goes against any reasonable logic, yet millions of people casually accept this theory and go about their lives, not considering their true destiny. If you do not believe in God but choose to follow these theories, good luck with your short stay on earth. Just one more thought: as you breathe your last breath and we all do, what next?

If there is a God

- There is a God, and he is all-powerful.
- There is a God, and he is all-knowing.
- There is a God, and he created the universe.
- There is a God. He created all human beings to his likeness and for his glory.
- There is a God. He created a magnificent reproductive system for everything living for the reason of procreation and pleasure.
- There is a God. He created the planetary system, the livable atmosphere, water, our earth, and everything in it.
- There is a God. He created all beauty and splendor of this planet from the tops of the highest mountains to the depths of the deepest seas.
- There is a God. He is a just God and a loving God. He gives us laws and commandments that he expects us to keep.
- There is a God. "For God so loved the world, that He gave his one and only Son, that whosoever believes in Him, shall not perish but have eternal life" (John 3:16).
- There is a God. His Son, Jesus, died on the cross to save us from our sins.
- There is a God, and he cannot tolerate sin.
- There is a God. Through Jesus Christ, all of our sins are forgiven, and we receive the gift of the Holy Spirit.
- There is a God, and he gives us free will. We choose to accept or reject him.

God is love with boundless mercy and forgiveness. With Jesus Christ as our Savior, presiding in our heart, we are promised eternity in heaven with God. There we have boundless joy, no sickness, no pain, and no misery, no hate, living in the glory of God in a new perfect body.

For me, God is the logical answer to that age-old question. It only makes sense. With Jesus presiding in my heart, that's the only proof I need. Reading God's Word daily, talking to God daily, hearing God daily, and being guided daily by the Holy Spirit leave no doubts in my mind. But the proof of God is irrefutable to his believers and they know where they will spend eternity. As I follow Jesus Christ, there's only truth, no tricks, no spin, and no contradictions. God has always been the same, the same today and the same for eternity. If you choose to believe in God, come to him with a sincere, humble heart. From your mouth, pray that you believe God sent his only Son to die on the cross, and He arose to save you from your sins. Ask God to forgive you for your sins. Ask this in Jesus' name, you will be saved and spend eternity with him in heaven. If you believe your life will change, a new journey will begin. As a believer, you will desire to follow God's will with your life and be more like Jesus Christ. Reading the Bible daily is the best way to learn God's will. Prayer daily asking for the knowledge of his will and the power to carry it out. Regularly attending a good Bible-based church is always a great way to improve spirituality.

Samuel was Hebrew originated meaning "God heard." God heard me and saved my mortal life. Now not only does God hear me, but he also speaks to me. Not only was my mortal life spared, but also my soul was saved for eternity in heaven.

In chapter 14, I quoted a scripture. This scripture was pointed out by God through the Holy Spirit while I was meditating.

It was John chapter 7, verses 14–18, in the New Testament:

> Not until halfway through the feast did Jesus go up to the temple courts and begin to teach. The Jews were amazed and asked, How did this man get such learning without having studied? Jesus answered, my teaching is not my own. It comes from Him who sent me. If anyone chooses to do God's will, he will find out whether my teaching comes from God or whether I speak on my own. He who speaks on his own does so to gain honor

of the one who sent him is a man of truth; there
is nothing false about him.

To me, the way I understand, speaking of or about the Scripture
is not as powerful as speaking exactly the words of the Bible as it is
written. There have been times when arguments cropped up with
people close to me.

I may have spoken falsely about God, believing I knew his word
when I didn't. Now I meant well. I didn't intentionally misinterpret
or mislead, but the results are the same.

If I'm incorrect while teaching God's Word, it hurts his king-
dom. These passages clarified this to me. I'm not Jesus, but I should
aspire to be more like him. This made it very clear to me the importance of knowing and understanding God's Word to the best of my
ability. These abilities don't come quick and easy, so that means I
need to put as much time as possible into reading God's Word with
prayer and meditation. I know God expects this from me and that's
the reason why these passages were presented to me.

Do you listen when God speaks to you?

Do you know how to recognize when God is speaking to you?

Ask God for a heart to hear, he does listen and he will speak to
you. I ask God that this book will bless all who read it. God is the
answer to everything. God has blessed me and my family despite all
of the wrongs which I have done. It doesn't matter to me what happens on this planet, this small amount of time I have here spend it
doing God's will to the best of my abilities I will do it with joy in my
heart knowing Jesus is with me always.

Whatever I accomplish or acquire, good or bad, I give all glory
to God, the Creator and the Master of the universe.

ABOUT THE AUTHOR

ONCE A YOUNG BOY, Sam was full of big dreams, high energy, and unstoppable drive and ambition. Difficult circumstances, some avoidable and some not, mixed with a mental disorder, topped off with early alcohol and substance abuse.

A life with adventures, successes, failures, death-defying actions, and miracles. Overexuberance for making big money and having excitement along with alcohol were the causes for irrational decision making and lone thinking.

It eventually led to big losses, destruction, family pain, death knocking at the door, hopelessness, and despair. It was time for major changes. Then through repentance, forgiveness, and redemption through Jesus Christ, Samuel, a new man, emerges. After rebuilding the wreckage of the past, Samuel now lives an exciting, fulfilling, sustainable, and a bright new future with God at the wheel.

CPSIA information can be obtained
at www.ICGtesting.com
Printed in the USA
JSHW051439200722
28260JS00002BA/112